The Story of Bermuda and Her People

The Story of Bermuda and Her People

W. S. ZUILL

Second Edition

MACMILLAN CARIBBEAN

First published 1973
Reprinted 1978
Second edition 1983

Published by
Macmillan Education
London and Basingstoke
Companies and representatives in Lagos, Zaria, Manzini,
Nairobi, Singapore, Hong Kong, Delhi, Dublin, Auckland,
Melbourne, Tokyo, New York, Washington, Dallas

ISBN 0 333 34156 2

Printed in Hong Kong

Contents

Contents (*continued*)

Foreword

by the Hon. Sir Edward Richards C.B.E., M.C.P., former Premier

This volume will occupy a place of honour among the many histori-cal works about Bermuda. Unlike many similar writings which deal only with segments of the past, this book, within the limitations of printed space, spans the period from 1609 up to recent times.

The author has peered into the mists of the past and has produced a work which is at once factual and imaginative. It is his theme that Bermuda's past was like its present: divisive forces were active and strong in the community but the forces which united the people were cohesive and stronger. Whether slave or free, black or white, Bermudians within their circumscribed area throughout the years faced nature's ravages together, lived through times of feast and famine together, died together when occasional epidemics swept the island and together repaired and rebuilt after the scourges and tempests had passed away.

We are more numerous today than yesterday and we cannot escape from each other. If the present is a reflection of the past then, despite the age-old divisive forces among us, the ties of togetherness which bind us will, as in the past, prevail.

The book is written in simple style, is informative and dates a num-ber of events of interest to all Bermudians. It may easily form the basis in the preparation of a 'nutshell' of Bermuda history for schools.

Introduction

In this book I have tried to look at the Bermuda people as a whole, not as white Bermudians and black Bermudians. We tend to see ourselves as split apart because a split exists, and existed more strongly in the past. But that very same past was shared by both groups, who worked for the island together, at the same tasks, and the theme of this work is that the experience of the past combined with the geographic, social and economic realities of today, are far more important than skin colour. Fortunately for the community many Bermudians feel this, and the result has been that the period after the Second World War has seen Bermuda undergo a vital transition in which the second-class citizenship which had been the lot of black people from Emancipation Day 1834, has virtually come to an end, though the result has not been achieved without a struggle.

At the time of writing Bermuda in many ways was showing the world how two groups of people of different skin colours could live together successfully. Although there had been surface indications of discord, our two most recent riots were almost entirely the work of youngsters, who received little tangible support from the rest of the island. By contrast, the general strike of 1981 was backed by workers of both races.

My first expression of thanks must go to the Hon. Sir Edward Richards, M.P., Bermuda's first Prime Minister under a 1973 change in the constitution, who was good enough to write the exceptionally kind foreword, as well as making suggestions about the manuscript.

The writing of this history could not have been achieved without the help of many people. First and foremost I would like to thank the late Dr Kenneth Robinson, Senior Education Officer, who suggested my name as author of a Bermuda history book, and was thereafter of the greatest help. His suggestion was taken up by Mr G. W. Lennox of Macmillan Education, who put his faith in my ability to produce the work, for which I am profoundly grateful.

I also relied on Dr Robinson's unpublished thesis on Bermuda education, and on his published work on the Berkeley Educational Society. Another unpublished thesis which was of great help was that of Mr Ottiwell Simmons, an official of the Bermuda Industrial Union, on the history of industrial trade unionism in Bermuda.

No work on Bermuda history would be complete without acknowledging the great debt Bermuda owes the late Dr Henry Wilkinson, whose four volumes covering the history of Bermuda from the seventeenth to the nineteenth century comprise the definitive history of our island. They are his enduring monument, and will give him an honoured place long after the community leaders of our time have passed from the memory of our grandchildren.

I would also like to acknowledge the general debt all island historians owe Major General Sir J. H. Lefroy, one-time Governor, whose *Memorials of the Bermudas* put the major part of the documents pertaining to Bermuda's early history in print.

Among the others who have helped me either through their published works or personally are Mrs Terry Tucker, whose knowledge of Bermuda history is encyclopaedic, Mr Leonard McDonald, the former Bermuda Archivist; the late Sister Jean de Chantal Kennedy; Mr Ian Ferguson, Miss Eva Hodgson, Mrs Albert Jackson, Dr the Hon. E. S. D. Ratteray, the late Mr Cyril Smith, Mr J. Wakefield and Mr James Williams and his staff at the Ministry of Tourism. On the geographical chapters I am particularly indebted to Mr David Lonsdale, Dr Walwyn Hughes, Mr Edward Manuel and Mrs David Wingate.

The responsibility for any errors is mine.

Finally I want to thank my mother and father for generating my interest in history and for much information, both verbal and through the pages of *Bermuda Journey* and *Bermuda Sampler*, and my brother for his help and backing.

But above all I wish to thank my wife for her encouragement, understanding, patience and help during the pressures of writing this volume.

W. S. Zuill
1st October 1981

List of Illustrations and Maps

Acknowledgments

The author and publishers wish to acknowledge the following sources of photographs:

Bermuda News Bureau, pp. 5, 6, 15, 16, 19, 22, 32, 33, 37, 47, 53, 56, 59, 63, 65, 74, 77, 87, 94, 100, 105, 118, 125, 126, 133, 139, 143, 153, 161, 181, 183, 189, 191, 195, 221, 222, 226 and the colour plates; Bermuda National Trust, pp. 15, 22, 87, 105, 168; Bermuda Historical Society, p. 19; Mansell Collection, p. xvi; Radio Times Hulton Picture Library, pp. 82, 103; Scottcraft, p. 193; cover Mr G. W. Lennox.

PROLOGUE

It had not been a stormy voyage, but when was it going to end?
Week after week the three small ships had sailed across the Atlantic,
constantly heading westward, pushed by the prevailing winds.
When would it end?

It took incredible courage to keep going into the unknown, into
seas which no one knew. At one stage the men's courage failed and
there was an attempt to make the Admiral turn back. He refused,
but soon he knew he would have to reverse his course, for supplies
were running low.

Then signs of land began to appear, branches and land birds.
At last, on 12th October 1492 the glad news rang out: '*Land*!'

It was an island and the Admiral, Christopher Columbus, named
it San Salvador. It was an outrider of many other islands and of the
great continent of America, which stretches from the Arctic Circle
almost to the Antarctic.

We now know that others had sailed across the Atlantic before
Columbus, but their achievements were forgotten. Before 1492 the
Atlantic was a great barrier; since then it has been a highway
between the continents.

That is why the story of Columbus is important to us in Bermuda, as it is to every part of the Americas. The way now was
open and not long after the Admiral set foot on San Salvador
Bermuda was also discovered.

Columbus on board his ship.

Columbus himself might well have discovered Bermuda on his homeward voyage. He sailed north from the Caribbean until he was close to our latitudes before he turned east to head back to Spain and a hero's welcome.

Part 1

Pre-Settlement Bermuda

CHAPTER 1

The Curtain Rises

Who discovered Bermuda and when they did is not clear. What is known is that in 1511 a map was published in an atlas called the *Legatio Babylonica*, which included Bermuda under the name *La Bermuda*. The Spanish historian Herrera says the island was discovered by Juan de Bermudez in command of a ship called *La Garza* (*The Heron*), but the first description of anyone visiting the island came only in 1515. That was the year Gonzales Ferdinando d'Oviedo sighted Bermuda and tried to land some pigs with the idea that they would become wild, and would be available as food for the crew of any ship which came close to the island or was wrecked. D'Oviedo failed to land the pigs because the wind was against him, but he later wrote a description of what Bermuda looked like.

The route Columbus took home on his first voyage became a favourite track for ships bound from the Caribbean to Spain. Sailing ships in those days were difficult to sail against the wind, and so the Spaniards needed a route where they were blown or pushed by favourable winds or currents. By sailing north up the Gulf Stream they were able to work themselves clear of the belt of easterly winds until they reached the latitude of Bermuda, where the winds are more likely to be westerly and helpful.

Bermuda stood alone amongst thousands of miles of ocean; there were no other islands or rocks in these latitudes, and the

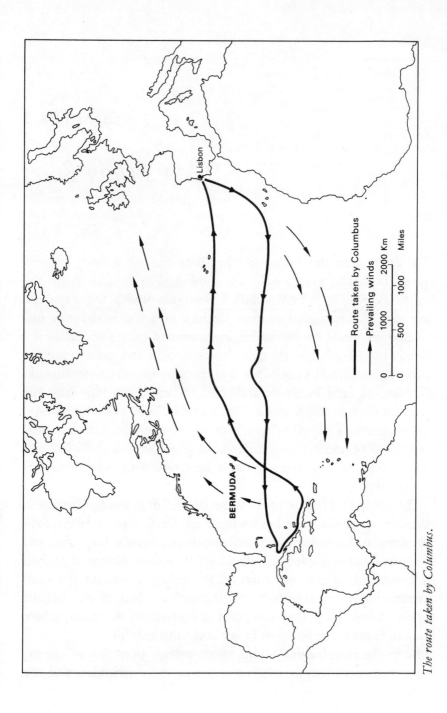

The route taken by Columbus.

navigators had to be extremely careful to avoid this tiny place, with its dangerous hidden reefs running out to sea. Not all ships succeeded, for sometimes navigators made mistakes, and sometimes storms drove ships onto Bermuda.

Mr Harry Cox with a Spanish astrolabe.

In recent times the discovery of aqualung diving equipment has made underwater exploration much easier, and although through the ages many Bermudians have dived to explore wrecks, much more has been discovered recently. Two Bermudian divers in particular, Teddy Tucker and Harry Cox, have made important finds in our reef-ridden waters. One of Mr Cox's finds was an astrolabe, which in the time we are talking about was one of the few instruments navigators had for obtaining a rough idea of their position.

Mr Teddy Tucker with treasure from a Spanish wreck, now on display in the Aquarium Museum.

The Portuguese and Bermuda

The Spanish who had discovered Bermuda made no attempt to settle there, but in 1527 the Portuguese nearly did so. A man from the Azores named Ferdinand Caemlo received permission to bring colonists to Bermuda, but as far as is known nothing came of it.

The first Portuguese arrived in 1543, some sixteen years later, and left behind a carving on a rock at Spittal Pond, Smith's Parish, a replica of which is there now. It is now known that in that year a Portuguese ship bound for Portugal from the city of Santo Domingo in the Caribbean was wrecked on Bermuda. Thirty-two men came safely ashore and built a ship in which they returned to Santo Domingo.

Many years later the rock carving was discovered, and was called Spanish Marks. The date was clear—1543—but the initials were not. They could have been R and a cross; but when the information about the Portuguese shipwreck reached Bermuda in recent years, it seemed likely that the carving was in fact a monogram of *RP*— Rex Portugaline—and the cross was a badge of the Portuguese Order of Christ. There can scarcely be any doubt now that the carving was made by a member of the ship's company, perhaps as he kept watch over the ocean hoping to see a vessel coming which would take them from the deserted island.

The carving itself no longer exists (a well-meaning attempt to save it resulted in its crumbling away) but a brass casting of it has been put in the same place. A plaster of Paris casting is on display in the Bermuda Historical Society museum in Hamilton.

Early French and English Visitors

The first French people to come to Bermuda also arrived because they were shipwrecked. This happened some time between 1560–70. Again a boat was made, and on this occasion the men sailed north to Newfoundland, where they probably met a vessel from the great cod fishing fleet which has congregated off the Grand Banks since 1500 or thereabouts, and perhaps even earlier.

The first known Englishman to visit here arrived on board a French ship in 1593. It was a dark night in December, and the ship drove on through the night. Her navigator had assured the captain that there was no danger of running into Bermuda. For this he was rewarded with liquor, known as his 'wine of height', for navigating the ship safely that far—and perhaps this had a bearing on what happened next, for as the ship drove on it suddenly struck a reef (perhaps North Rock) which towered out of the water.

The crew built a raft, but even so there was room for only half of them on the raft and in the ship's boat. The Englishman, Henry May, hesitated to get in the boat, but Captain de la Barbotière told him to get aboard, and after many hours of rowing they came safely to the shore. It seems likely that the rest of the crew were saved later. A ship was built, which took them all to Newfoundland and the Grand Banks, where they found a passage home.

The Story of Venturilla

The first known black man to come to Bermuda was called Venturilla and he arrived on board a Spanish ship commanded by Captain Diego Ramirez. Ramirez was skipper of one of five treasure galleons homeward bound for Spain. Early in the voyage they ran into a storm, and Captain Ramirez' ship struck the rocks of Bermuda. Luckily for them all, the ship was forced across the reefs and into Great Sound.

When Ramirez' ship anchored in the bay night was falling and the captain sent a small boat ashore to find water. Darkness crept over the land, and, as happens today, birds started chattering; but there were many more birds then. One bird song probably that of the shearwater, sounded to the Spanish like 'Diselo, diselo', which means 'Tell 'em' in English.

A seaman on the ship said: 'What is this devil trying to tell me? Out with it! Let us hear what it is!'

Captain Ramirez, remembering all the seamen's tales about devils living on Bermuda, and about the island being enchanted, said: 'Ah; these are the devils of Bermuda, which they say are hereabouts. The sign of the Cross at them! We are Christians!'

The captain's words probably frightened the seamen a bit more, and just at that moment the small boat shot back alongside. The men clambered up the side of the ship exclaiming: 'What devils are these? The boat's rudder is broken!'

Captain Ramirez by now was in better control of himself, and ordered another rudder to be made immediately, because the boat would have to be used in the morning to search for water, and without a rudder it would be difficult to handle.

He ordered Venturilla to go ashore and cut a piece of wood for a new rudder. Despite his fears, Venturilla obeyed. Perhaps, as his name suggests, he was eager for adventure. He landed with his lantern and disappeared in the bushes. Then he began to yell.

Ramirez shouted: 'The devil is carrying off the negro! All ashore!'

Men tumbled into the boat and rapidly rowed ashore, where they too began to yell as unseen enemies rushed at them out of the dark. As they hit and clubbed, one or two men with cooler heads discovered the attackers were not devils, but birds, and were probably good to eat, too. So they killed 500 of them, brought them to the ship, cooked them and enjoyed them very much; indeed, they lived off them most of the rest of their stay in Bermuda.

Captain Ramirez drew a map of the island and also set up a large cross with directions on it in Spanish telling future visitors where to find drinking water. This was later mistaken by English settlers as an indication of buried treasure. Remains of a camp have been found, and ever since the area has been known as Spanish Point.

The next known shipwreck was a momentous one for Bermuda, because it led to the settlement of these islands by Britain some 350 years ago. This story is told in the next chapter.

NOTE

Ancient legends tell of an Irish monk named St Brendan sailing around the Atlantic in the mid-sixth century, and there is reason to think that one of the legends refers to Bermuda. The legend tells of an island with birds chattering at sunset, an isolated island far from any other land, discovered by St Brendan on a voyage in which he was accompanied by other monks.

Whether St Brendan actually existed and did all that he is credited with is an unanswered historical question. It may be that Irish monks did sail across the Atlantic and return to tell the tale; the ocean has been crossed a number of times in cockleshells, including rowboats. But whether St Brendan was actually involved in any of these voyages is another question.

What the truth is we are never likely to know, but these ancient legends should not be completely dismissed.

The St Brendan story is commemorated in Bermuda by the use of his name for a hospital and a pilot boat; one of the dioramas at Fort St Catherine depicts the monk and his companions on a boat.

CHAPTER 2

The Great Storm

In the year 1610 William Strachey sat down at a crude table in a hut in Jamestown, Virginia, to write the story of a notable shipwreck, how a ship's company had been saved, and how they had fared on an uninhabited island. Dipping his quill pen into the ink, he began with the sailing of a fleet from England the year before.

Seven ships and two smaller vessels, called pinnaces, gathered at Plymouth to carry supplies and colonists to the tiny, weak English settlement up the James River from Chesapeake Bay which had been started just two years before. This was the nucleus from which the great English-speaking United States was to grow, but it was so small and poor a nucleus that time and time again it was barely saved.

The largest ship in the fleet was the *Sea Venture*, 300 tons, broad in the beam, built to carry goods and people safely over the dangerous sea. She was the flagship, and aboard her were the Admiral of the fleet, Sir George Somers; the Deputy Governor of Jamestown, Sir Thomas Gates; the Captain of the ship, Christopher Newport (who had headed the first expedition to Jamestown); and Strachey, who was Gates' secretary.

There were lots of other people aboard too. There were gentlemen—one in particular named Henry Paine. There was a wealthy lady, Mistress Horton, and her maid. There was a priest, the Rev Richard Bucke. There was a man who one day was to discover how to cure Virginia tobacco so that it was pleasant for English tastes, and who was also to marry the Indian Princess Pocahontas. He was John Rolfe, and he was on the *Sea Venture* with his first wife, who was soon to have a baby.

Also aboard were two men who were not going to Virginia to settle but who were going home. They were Indians named Matchumps and Namuntuck, and they had been persuaded to go to England by Captain John Smith, that amazing and extraordinary adventurer who at this time was holding the Virginia colony together.

There were also working people and sailors, probably all white, though there is no reason to suppose that there should not have been black people among them too.

Plymouth, at the mouth of the English Channel, was a good place to start for the Americas, and on 2nd June 1609 the fleet set sail. Under Sir George Somers' orders they set a course south until they reached a position south of Bermuda and then they headed across the Atlantic. Taking this route was a big change; previously Captain Newport had followed the old trade route right down to the Caribbean before heading north towards Virginia.

The voyage went well. The fleet stayed together, and day after day the vessels made progress. Each day the sun came up, revealing nothing but sea all around. The sails bellied, the wind whistled through the rigging, the water constantly bubbled and hissed as it slid along the hulls, and the wooden ribs and planking creaked as the ships' rose and fell in the long Atlantic waves.

The only incident was that one of the smaller vessels, a pinnace, turned back to England. The other pinnace was towed by the *Sea Venture* so that her slow speed would not delay the fleet.

Then on a day when Captain Newport estimated that they were about a week away from Chesapeake Bay, the weather changed, and, as evening grew to darkness heavy clouds covered the sky, hiding the stars. When dawn came the waves had become steeper and more menacing and the wind was singing a new and more

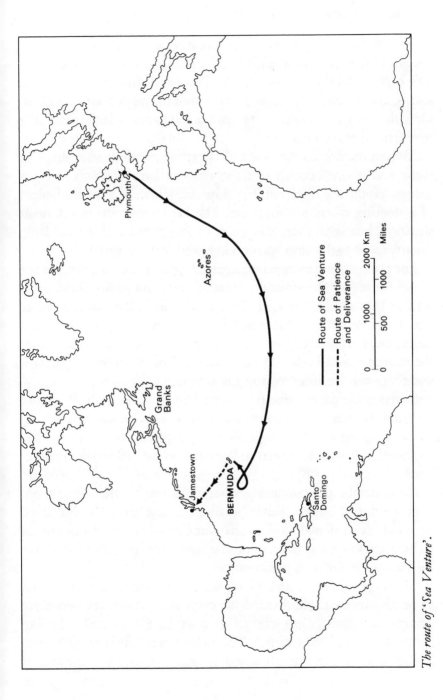

The route of 'Sea Venture'.

sinister note in the rigging. The weather made it dangerous for the *Sea Venture* to continue towing the pinnace, and she was cast off. The captains of the ships soon had their hands full coping with the storm, and quickly the vessels disappeared from one another's sight. Only the *Sea Venture* and the pinnace failed to reach Jamestown; the rest arrived there safely.

Aboard the *Sea Venture* the sails were now furled; an attempt to show even a small corner of canvas meant that it took six to eight men to handle the tiller and the whipstaff, which was the equivalent of a steering wheel in those days. The *Sea Venture* was in a difficult situation, but soon there was more to fear when a sailor suddenly discovered that the ship was leaking, and leaking badly.

The pumps were manned immediately, and the crew searched the vessel for leaks. They found a great number and stuffed them up as well as they could, using cloth and even beef, but still the water poured in. What had happened was that the fierce waves of the hurricane had battered the planking, pulling and pressing it so that the movement had released the caulking from between the planks, and there was nothing to stop the water.

It was a desperate situation. The ship was alone, rolling and pitching, helpless in the enormous waves. The sea was pouring in. '. . . to me,' Strachey wrote at his table in Jamestown, 'this leakage appeared as a wound, given to men that were before [*i.e.* already] dead.'

He remembered wondering whether it was worth fighting on. 'Yet we did,' he said, 'either because so dear are a few lingering hours of life in all mankind, or that our Christian knowledge taught us how much we owed . . . not to be false to ourselves or to neglect the means of our own preservation . . .'

At this point Sir Thomas Gates showed why he had been chosen to be a Governor. He divided the crew and passengers into three groups, and each group worked away at the pumps and at bailing for an hour, and then rested. The bailing was hard; small barrels had to be filled with water below decks and hoisted from one person

Sir Thomas Gates.

to another up to the main deck to be poured out. Both Sir Thomas and Sir George Somers took part in the work, although Sir George was also busy overseeing the steering and attempting to ease the ship's way through the harsh and cruel sea.

One enormous wave broke over the stern; water filled the centre section. The shock knocked men off their feet and made Strachey think the *Sea Venture* was gone; but slowly the ship rose up and continued her mad career northward, a plaything of both wind and wave.

The storm hit on Tuesday, 25th June and the leak started the same day. By Thursday the men's muscles and spirits were flagging as they continued their desperate day and night battle against the in-pouring sea. That night St Elmo's fire appeared in the rigging; Strachey calls it 'an apparition of a little round light, like a faint star, trembling and streaming along with a sparkling blaze, half the height upon the mainmast, and shooting sometimes from shroud to shroud . . . and for three or four hours together . . . it kept with us, running sometimes along the mainyard to the very end and then returning.'

It was frightening to some of the crew, but Strachey and a number of others knew that this phenomenon occurred sometimes in storms. We know now that it is an electrical discharge, a sort of mini-lightning.

This reconstruction shows survivors of the 'Sea Venture' wreck struggling ashore at St Catherine's Beach.

When dawn came on Friday the storm seemed just as bad, and the ship's company were giving up the struggle. In a desperate attempt to keep the ship afloat they started to lighten her, throwing trunks and stores overboard, and even the ship's starboard guns. The morning wore on, and all around was the waste of waters. Then, as more men gave up hope, stopped bailing, and lay down to rest, Sir George Somers sighted land.

It was Bermuda.

There were trees waving in the fierce wind, and the sight gave the passengers and crew new courage. They started bailing the *Sea Venture* again. Sails were set and the ship drove eastward down the South Shore, slowly working in closer to land. Finally they reached St David's Head, and rounded to, protected from the wind and sea, but the *Sea Venture* was still leaking as badly as ever. Then Sir George ordered the ship to be headed for shore, and after travelling another mile the vessel bumped over a reef and stuck fast between two rocks. Her remains are in the vicinity to this day.

Sir Thomas Gates jumped into the first boat, as was his right as land commander, and went ashore. As he reached the land (at St Catherine's beach) he shouted 'Gates, his bay!'

During the afternoon the *Sea Venture*'s boats plied back and forth, and by nightfall everyone was safe ashore. They were safe, but now they faced dangers from each other.

NOTE

There have been many theories about the course of the *Sea Venture* in the storm and what part of Bermuda Sir George Somers sighted. The theory used here is that of Mr Cyril Smith, who also made the plans and model of the *Deliverance* from which the full-scale replica in St George's was made (see next chapter).

CHAPTER 3

Mutinies and Murders

From the start Sir George and Sir Thomas did not get on well together. Sir George, who was known as 'a lamb on shore but a lion at sea' had been in supreme command on the *Sea Venture*, but on shore Sir Thomas, as the future Deputy Governor, was in charge. Sea commanders and shore commanders have often disagreed and in their disagreement caused a great deal of trouble, and this was one of the reasons why the *Sea Venture* people did not have a happy time on the island.

The ship's company stayed in Bermuda for nine months before they completed the construction of two small ships and sailed safely to Virginia. One of these was the *Deliverance*. Exactly what she looked like we do not know, but Strachey gives her size and from what he said and from a knowledge of ships of the time a full-scale replica has been built by the Junior Service League at St George's. The replica gives us a good idea not only of the *Deliverance* but also of ships of the seventeenth century in general.

The original *Deliverance* was built under the direction of the *Sea Venture*'s carpenter, Richard Frobisher, and the bay at which he built her was named Frobisher's Building's Bay. Today it is still called Buildings Bay.

The other vessel was called the *Patience*. She was built under the supervision of Sir George somewhere on the mainland away from the main camp. The *Patience* was built entirely of Bermuda cedar

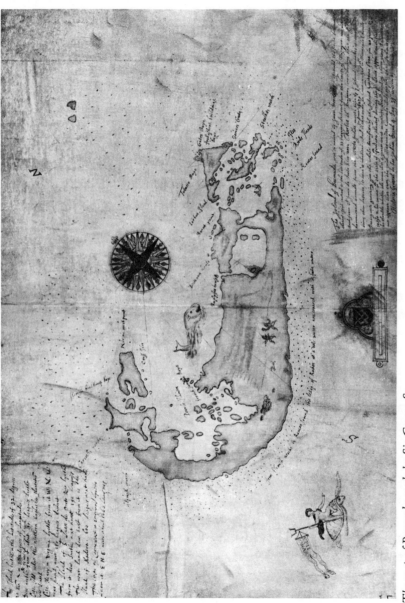

The map of Bermuda made by Sir George Somers.

with only one iron bolt (taken from the *Sea Venture*), while the ribs of the *Deliverance* and much of the rest of the vessel were made from materials taken from the wreck.

When the *Sea Venture* company came ashore Sir George busied himself with fishing for food while Sir Thomas worried about sending a boat to get help from Virginia. The *Sea Venture*'s biggest boat, the longboat, was fitted with a deck; eight men boarded her, with Master's Mate Henry Ravens in command, and set sail for Virginia.

Ravens calculated he would be back in a month, and in September Strachey was put in charge of a bonfire built on St David's Head and set to keep watch for the longboat. He spent two months watching, but Ravens and his men never reached Jamestown and were never seen again.

After Ravens sailed away Sir George took a boat and explored Bermuda, creating a remarkably accurate map, an ancient copy of which still exists and is in the archives in Hamilton (see page 19). Sir George's map is illustrated with four pictures, two of them fanciful, and two of them showing men getting food by fishing and by hunting. The hunters are accompanied by the ship's dog and are hunting pigs, which they found in great abundance, thanks either to some Spanish captain like d'Oviedo or to a shipwreck. At the time the *Sea Venture* was wrecked the pigs were fat from eating cedar and palmetto berries; later they lost their fat when the berry season ended. Then the settlers started living on turtles and later cahows (sea birds) and, of course, fish. They also used the *Sea Venture*'s stores, but these were carefully rationed.

When Ravens sailed away Sir Thomas ordered work to be started on the *Deliverance*, and he himself laboured as hard as anyone. But many of the passengers and crew did not like the hard work, such as hewing down cedar trees and cutting them into planks with hand saws and said: 'Why don't we just stay here, where there is lots of food and not much work to do to get it?'

A man named Nicholas Bennet was the first to start talking in this way, and he soon persuaded a small group that he was right.

One of his followers was Christopher Carter, who in fact never did leave Bermuda; he was the first settler, and later became Governor for a short time. Many Bermudians living today are descended from him.

Sir Thomas sent Bennet and his followers to live on a small island by themselves, but pretty soon they found they did not like it, and Sir Thomas allowed them to return.

The second mutiny was a one-man affair. A person named Stephen Hopkins, who was a man of considerable education also wanted to stay on the island. Sir Thomas ordered Hopkins to be shot, but, says Strachey, 'So penitent he was, and made so much moan, alleging the ruin of his wife and children in this his trespass, as it wrought in the hearts of all the better sort of the company, who therefore with humble entreaties and earnest supplications went unto our Governor . . .' Sir Thomas relented, and Hopkins survived to return to England and go out to America again in 1620 aboard the *Mayflower*.

The third mutiny could have been by far the most serious. A group of men planned to kill the Governor, seize the storehouse and make off with whatever tools and food they needed. Most of those involved were helping to build the *Patience* under the command of Sir George. Sir Thomas heard about the plot and ordered every man to carry a weapon with him at all times. He also doubled the night watch. This prevented the conspirators taking any action but everyone remained uneasy.

Then on one evening, 13th March, Henry Paine, one of the conspirators, was ordered to go on watch. He refused, with a good deal of rudeness, and the next day was tried and sentenced to be hanged immediately. Paine confessed what he had been up to, and asked, since he was a gentleman, to be shot instead of hanged, 'and toward evening', says Strachey, 'he had his desire, the sun and his life setting together.'

News of Paine's execution reached Sir George's boat-building camp and many of the twenty men who were with him immediately

Sir George Somers.

ran away into the woods for fear that Paine had given their names as being involved in the plot (in fact he had not). Not only that; they also asked Sir Thomas for a store of meal and clothing.

Did Sir George sympathise with them? Strachey does not say so, but reading between the lines it seems likely. The conspirators were probably all sailors, not passengers, and there is reason to think that

Sir George had a special feeling for them. Also, it is obvious that Sir George himself had fallen in love with Bermuda and was not anxious to leave.

By this time Sir George and Sir Thomas were not very friendly with each other, but the danger of mutiny was so serious that Sir Thomas decided to try and heal the breach. He wrote a long letter to Sir George, urging him to try and reach the runaway seamen and 'by the virtue of that ancient love and friendship, which has these many years been settled between them, to do his best' to make the men return to their duty.

Sir George was moved by the letter, and in the end succeeded in bringing back all the sailors except Christopher Carter and Robert Waters. Waters was a murderer; he had killed another seaman named Edward Samuell with a shovel, and had been sentenced to death, but his fellow sailors had helped him escape. Carter did not return because he was convinced that, having rebelled twice, he would be punished by Sir Thomas.

There was another murder, a secret one. John Smith tells about it: '. . . some . . . differences fell betweene them, that Matchumps slew Namuntuck, and having made a hole to bury him, because it was too short, he cut off his legs and laid them by him, which murder he concealed till he was in Virginia.'

During the stay on the island two children were born, a girl named Bermuda and a boy named Bermudas. Bermuda was the daughter of John Rolfe, but she died here soon after she was born.

After all their troubles the two small vessels sailed from Bermuda on 12th May, leaving Carter and Waters behind.

Rescue at Jamestown

The *Patience* and *Deliverance* took only ten days to reach Chesapeake Bay, and soon afterwards were working their way up the James River to Jamestown. The settlement was in a shocking state. Only sixty people were alive, supplies had nearly run out, and the *Sea*

Venture survivors from Bermuda, instead of finding help after all their troubles, became the rescuers of the colony.

Although the *Patience* and *Deliverance* brought good supplies of food, there was not enough to keep the whole of Jamestown going, so it was decided to abandon the colony, using two pinnaces already at hand and the two Bermuda-built vessels. They thought they would sail to the Grand Banks for help and a passage to England.

On 7th June Jamestown was abandoned and the fleet set sail down the river. On the same day a new supply fleet, with the Governor of Virginia, Lord De La Warr, aboard, was putting into the mouth of the river. The vessels met, and all put back to Jamestown.

Even then the supply situation was not greatly improved, and Sir George offered to go back to Bermuda in the *Patience* to obtain more food. On 19th June he set sail, accompanied by Captain Samuel Argall who was Deputy Governor of Virginia. They set a course northward, planning to obtain fish before going to Bermuda, but in foggy weather the two vessels lost sight of each other. Sir George came on to Bermuda, but Captain Argall returned to Jamestown.

In Bermuda Sir George died and his nephew, Matthew Somers, decided to sail the *Patience* back to England rather than return to Virginia as Sir George wanted. He left behind Carter and Waters, who were joined by a third man, Edward Chard.

Matthew took Sir George's body with him, leaving the heart buried in Bermuda. When he finally arrived he and his crew told many tales about Bermuda, and letters arriving from Virginia confirmed what they said. This aroused tremendous interest, and the Virginia Company decided to send colonists to the island, as will be related later.

NOTE

Mementoes of Sir George   There are a few relics left of Sir George Somers. The one that tells the most about him is his own modest account of the wreck of the *Sea Venture*, given here in part. He wrote it to the Earl of Salisbury from Jamestown.

Right honourable:

May it please your good honour to be advised that since our departure out of England in going to Virginia about some 200 leagues from the Bermudas we were taken with a very great storm or hurricane which sundered all the fleet and on St James's Day being the 23rd of July we had such a leak in our ship insomuch that there was nine foot of water before we knew of any such thing. We pumped with two pumps and bailed in three or four places with certain barricoes and then we kept a hundred men always working night and day from the 23rd until the 28th of the same July, being Friday, at which time we saw the island of Bermuda, where our ship lieth upon the rock, a quarter of a mile distant from the shore where we saved all our lives and afterwards saved much of our goods, but all our bread was wet and lost.

We continued in the island from the 28th July until the 10th of May, in which time we built two small barques to carry our people to Virginia, which in number were 140 men and women at the coming to the island.

We departed from Bermuda 12th of May and arrived in Virginia the 23rd of the same month and coming to Cape Henry the captain there told us of the famine that was at Jamestown, whereupon we hastened up there and found it true, for they had eaten all the quick things that were there and some of them had eaten snakes or adders.

But by the industry of our Governor in the Bermudas [Sir Thomas Gates] there was saved a little meal . . . and [we] recovered all saving three that did die and were past recourse before our coming.

We consulted together what course were best to be taken for our means would not continue above fourteen days.

We thought good to take into our four pinnaces as much of the munition as we could and took in all the people and were going down the river but by the way we met with the Lord Delawar . . . which made our hearts very glad, and we presently returned up to Jamestown and there we found no savages for they were afraid to come thither . . .

Now we are in good hope to plant and abide here for here is a good course taken and a greater care than ever there was.

I am going to the Bermudas for fish and hogs with two small pinnaces and am in a good opinion to be back again before the Indians do gather their harvest.

Bermuda is the most plentiful place that ever I came to, for fish, hogs and fowl.

Thus wishing all health with the increase of honour I do humbly take my leave from Virginia . . .

Your honours to command
George Somers

Other mementoes of Sir George which have come down the ages are his lodestone (used to magnetise compass needles) and portraits of himself and his wife in the Bermuda Historical Society museum.

A portrait of Sir Thomas Gates is in the care of the Bermuda National Trust.

Part 2

The Archipelago

CHAPTER 4

The First Beginnings

When the Spanish sailors first found Bermuda jutting out of the broad expanses of the Atlantic the group of islands had already been in existence a long time. The island first began to form over seventy million years ago, at least, and probably well before that. Scientists are still trying to work out how long Bermuda and its underlying foundation, an extinct volcano, have been in existence. This enquiry is still continuing, and the ideas presented in these pages may undergo changes as more is discovered.

The present belief is that Bermuda started as one of a chain of volcanoes, for scientific exploration of the bottom of the Atlantic reveals that there are other, smaller mountains within 400 miles of this archipelago. The Bermuda mountain is the largest, rising steeply from the bottom of the sea.

But the above water island we know today does not contain volcanic rocks; they lie below sea-level buried by a cap of stone formed from tiny coral creatures. The coral creatures, the most important of which are called foraminifera, swarmed around the original submarine volcano mountain top, lived and died, leaving behind their countless millions of shells which gradually created a new layer of sand and rock. Millions of years passed, and a 250 foot thick cap of limestone from the shells covered the volcanic rock.

The world then passed into a period of time which scientists call the Pleistocene era, and in the long, long history of the world it is close to our own time—between one million and 20,000 years ago. The first known men appeared during the Pleistocene, and it was also the time of the great ice ages, which played an important part in the formation of Bermuda. For reasons which are still not known, the earth grew very much colder at least four, probably five times, during the Pleistocene. Each time great sheets of ice developed, locking up the supply of water so that the level of the oceans fell.

The lowering of the sea level each time exposed far more of the mountain-top and its coral cap. This appears to have resulted in the laying down of different layers of rock; the layers can be seen in cuttings, with the grain of the rock running in different directions, sometimes one layer separated from another by red soil or sand.

This rock was formed, it is now thought, during both the ice ages and the warm periods in between. Rain and wind and waves broke up the shells of the coral creatures, forming sand. The sand was taken by the wind and blown into hills, called dunes. Rain water dripped through these hills, sometimes washing the sand into valleys where it mixed with dust falling from the air to form soil, and sometimes working through the sand, causing a chemical action which cemented the sand together, forming the stone we know today. It is named aeolian limestone after the Greek god of the winds, Aeolus, because the wind helped to make it.

The coral creatures are still at work today, and dunes are still to be seen. During the late nineteenth century one moving dune at Elbow Beach even covered a cottage. Some people believe that the great reefs at the West End of Bermuda are still producing sand. They believe the prevailing south-west winds move the sand along the South Shore, so there is always a fresh supply for the beaches when the older sand is moved right over the edge of Mount Bermuda by heavy gales.

The Elbow Beach dune is one of the small changes which have occurred since man came to Bermuda, but there are others. There is reason to think, for instance, that North Rock was much higher above sea level when Henry May was wrecked a little over 400 years ago. Under the water at Shelly Bay you can still see the remains of a road which once ran across dry land.

The biggest change we know of however was caused by man, in 1941, when the United States built an airfield on St David's, Cooper's and other islands. Sand was sucked up from the bottom of the sea, hills were torn down, and the land was massively re-shaped into an airfield.

However the essential Bermuda that the Spanish sailors found appears to have been completed at the end of the last ice age of the Pleistocene. When the ice melted and the sea rose the valleys were drowned and only the higher hilltops remained above the water. These were concentrated on the southern and western sides of the mountain top, leaving underwater the shallow areas of the northern lagoon and the western reefs. Within the higher hills were three major basins: Great Sound and Castle Harbour, which are believed to be the craters through which the ancient volcano spewed its lava, and Harrington Sound.

Buried even deeper were two smaller tops of mountains, named the Argus and Challenger Banks after the ships which discovered them. Argus is some forty-two feet underwater, while Challenger is only about twenty-four feet underwater.

Today these banks make good fishing grounds. Argus has also been put to another purpose: a Texas Tower on four long legs was erected on the bank by the U.S. Navy for experiments in underwater submarine detection. The tower has now outlived its use and has been taken down.

Geography of Bermuda

The first mappers and explorers of Bermuda were struck by the large number of islands and islets, and it is still said today that the Bermuda archipelago, counting in a good many pinpoints of barely dry land, has 365 islands, one for every day of the year.

One of the few remaining cedars.

Some distinctive Bermudian sights.

Easter lilies; Bermuda's last export crop.

A long-tail peers from its nest in the cliffs.

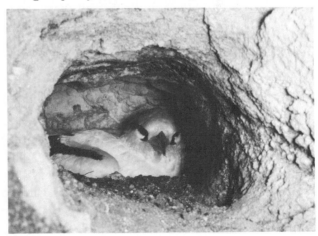

The major hills in Bermuda are found along the South Shore, running from Tucker's Town right onto Somerset Island. A lesser spine of hills goes along the North Shore, from Spanish Point along the northern edge of Harrington Sound, being picked up again on the northern side of St George's Island.

A surprising aspect of Bermuda are the number of caves, ranging in size from the Crystal and Leamington caves to the small ones found all over the island. Caves may be responsible for some of the valleys and coves. It is believed that caves are formed by wind pressure and water seepage working on weak spots. Sometimes though, when the weaker stone or sand has been scoured out the the roof itself collapses, leaving a valley or a cove or even perhaps a marsh.

Many of the caves which remain are remarkably beautiful, with colourful shining stalactites reaching down from the roof, and stalagmites reaching up from the floor. They are formed by drops of rainwater seeping through the red soil and stone covering the roof. The drops pick up minute quantities of material and leave some behind as they slip from the ceiling to tinkle down to the floor. There the remainder of the material is left, and slowly the stalagmites and stalactites grow toward each other as the drops form stone icicles and hillocks of what is known as driprock.

Trees and Plants

Bermuda is a fertile island covered by vegetation, except where rock heads break through the soil. The trees, bushes and plants have changed considerably since the first man came, for ever since the island was settled men have introduced new species, and now Bermuda has a sampling of flora from many different parts of the world.

Because Bermuda is an isolated island, over 600 miles from any other point of land, some varieties of trees and plants developed which are found nowhere else. These endemic plants include the cedar, which once covered the island with a cool, dark green forest. An insect pest which struck in 1945 destroyed nearly all the trees, but some still live. Whether they will ever dominate the island again is very questionable.

Another endemic is the olivewood bark, which fortunately is not now as rare as it was, many people having taken the trouble to cultivate this lovely but slow-growing tree.

Two plants which were long thought to be endemic but which are now considered to be only native are the palmetto and the Bermudiana, a little blue flower which appears in the grass in springtime. Native plants are ones which reached Bermuda on their own, without the aid of man, as seeds floating on the ocean, borne on the wind or carried by birds.

A number of trees have sprung up or have been planted to take the place of the cedars. Prominent among them are the all-spice or pimento, whose leaves and seeds make a useful flavouring; the fiddlewood, whose leaves turn red in both autumn and spring; the Surinam cherry whose red berries are a delight to children and adults, and which can be used to make delicious jellies and jams; the casuarina, which was planted in large numbers in the 1940s and 1950s as a replacement for the cedar; the tall Norfolk Island pine which stands out because of its height; and among the palms the hardy coconut and column-like royal.

Bermuda fruit trees include Canary Island bananas, loquats, guavas and a wide variety of citrus.

Queen of the Bermuda flowers is the Easter lily, which is Bermuda's last agricultural export. Common flowering shrubs throughout Bermuda are the oleander, often grown as a hedge, and the large hibiscus, which can be grown as a shrub, a tree or a hedge.

Morning glory or bluebell is a vine flower which grows cheerfully almost everywhere, while many Bermuda gardens have considerable plantings of geraniums. On the seashore can be found the wild prickly pear, with yellow flowers and a pleasant tasting red fruit, which must be peeled to get rid of the prickles before eating.

Among the ferns of interest are two endemic varieties, the pretty maidenhair and the tough sword fern. The green grass of Bermuda is known to all Bermudians as crab grass, but in the United States it is known as St Augustine grass.

Land Creatures and Birds

Bermuda has few wild animals, which is hardly surprising in view of the size of the island. The largest are rats. Houses often have little lizards running through them, eating flies and insects. These creatures are not native to Bermuda. The older, native lizards, known as skinks, rarely enter a house and are difficult to find.

Large, saucer-sized toads live in the fields and wander onto the roads. These were introduced to Bermuda by Captain Nathaniel Vesey in 1885 to help control pests. Bermuda also has the tiny whistling frog, which arrived at about the same time. The whistling frogs live in stone walls and in the bark of trees, and sing on summer nights and in the daytime after rain.

The only poisonous land creature in Bermuda is the centipede, which is rarely found. Centipedes are usually three to four inches long, equipped with numerous legs, and painful and poisonous pincers.

Much more common are several varieties of spiders, butterflies, moths, houseflies and mosquitoes, although the flies and mosquitoes are nowadays far fewer in number than they were. Bermuda once suffered from *aedes egyptii*, the mosquito which is the carrier of yellow fever, but these were eliminated in a campaign which started during the Second World War.

One of the prettiest sights in a summer sky is the soaring black and white longtail or tropic bird sailing over the warm sea ready to dive into the water to catch a fish. The longtail is one of the few species of birds which regularly visit Bermuda.

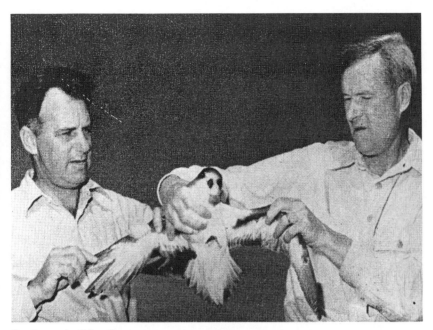

Re-discovery of the cahow.

A bird which is rarely seen and indeed is almost extinct is the cahow, which lived here in such large numbers before man came to settle in Bermuda, and helped to feed the *Sea Venture* company. The rediscovery of cahows, living on isolated islands in Castle Harbour, by Dr R. C. Murphy and Mr Louis Mowbray in 1951, has led to a major effort to increase the numbers of wide-ranging sea birds, with Mr David Wingate, Government Conservation Officer, in the forefront of the work. The cahows raise their young in burrows in the ground, and are therefore almost defenceless against attacks by dogs and rats, so that while Mr Wingate hopes to increase the species considerably, they are most unlikely to return to their pre-settlement numbers.

The principal birds are the black cat bird, the yellow-breasted kiskadee, the European sparrow, the cardinal or redbird, the American crow, the ground dove and the starling.

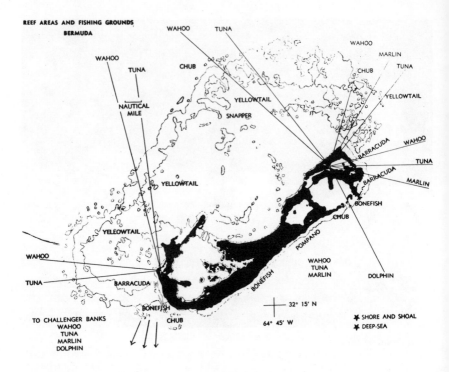

A Department of Tourism map indicating the main fishing grounds.

Bermuda Sea Creatures

Silvanus Jourdan, in the first book published in England about the wreck of the *Sea Venture*, was ecstatic about the number of Bermuda fish. 'Sir George Summers', he says, '. . . presently by his careful industry went and found out sufficient of many kinds of fishes, and so plentiful thereof that in half an hour he took so many fishes with hooks as did suffice the whole company one day. And fish is there so abundant that if a man step into the water, they will come round about him, so that men were fain to get out for fear of biting.

'These fish are very fat and sweet, and of the proportion and bigness that three of them will conveniently lade two men; those we called rockfish.'

After nearly 400 years of fishing in Bermuda waters, the fish are not quite so plentiful today, but the rockfish is still one of the principal sea creatures used for food.

In springtime humpback whales come to Bermuda waters to feed and raise their young before migrating further, and other species of whale pass by the island and occasionally come ashore. Right up to the beginning of the present century whaling was a Bermuda industry, and old whaling implements and carvings from whale bones are still to be seen.

Bermuda fish are most easily divided into two sections: the inshore fish found round about the reefs and on the Argus and Challenger Banks, and the oceanic or pelagic fish which roam the Atlantic and are generally found in the deep ocean.

Along the coastlines it is easy to find striped sergeant majors or cowpilots, small, brightly coloured fish which are expert at sneaking a bait off a hook. Also common are the grey bream with a black dot on the tail, and the small, silver-green fry—there are three main species—which are much prized as bait. The fry often leap from the water if pursued by enemies, particularly mackerels and jacks.

Harder to find are the shy angel fish, which are found nowhere else in the world. The angel fish are a deep blue colour, with bright yellow fins and piping. Colourful parrot fish can often be seen by snorkelers, and a favourite shallow water gamefish is the bonefish, which can be counted on to put up a good fight when hooked.

In deeper water are rockfish, varieties of snapper, hamlet, grouper, mackerel and yellowtail. Also found sometimes is the whipray, which has a bad but undeserved reputation. Further out at sea are the great Allison and blackfin tuna, dolphins and wahoo.

The principal hazard to swimmers are the various species of jellyfish, which sting, and the Portuguese man-of-war, which scientists believe to be several creatures living together, the main one the floating blue balloon, the long stinging tentacles being several others. The tentacles can deliver an intense sting and should be avoided. Another hazard around coral reefs is red fire or ginger coral, which can give a painful rash.

Bigger creatures which are feared by many people are the varieties of sharks and barracudas. Divers should watch for the Moray eels which live in crevices in the reefs. The principal danger comes from poking a hand into a cranny, for if a Moray is there he is capable of giving a severe bite.

CHAPTER 5

The Sea and the Weather

Far down to the south of Bermuda a hurricane is spawning. Out in the Atlantic, not far north of the equator, some force—and no one is quite sure how it starts—causes hot air to rise from the surface of the water. As the upwind continues the pressure of the air on the earth lightens in that spot, causing a small area of what weather forecasters call low pressure.

Because the atmosphere constantly tries to even the pressure, air rushes into the low pressure area or eye, and in its turn moves up the warm air column. The turning earth gradually creates a spinning motion and now the small beginning develops into an enormous storm.

The storm has winds which reach out for 200 miles or more. Clouds gather, and nowadays these are recorded by weather satellites circling the globe high above the atmosphere. The satellites send their signals to receiving stations on earth—there is one at the U.S. Naval Air Station in Bermuda—and these convert the satellite signals into maps showing the cloud cover over a vast area of the Atlantic.

The circular nature of the hurricane makes it easy to spot, for its clouds look like a great spiral. Aircraft are sent to measure the storm and its intensity. By parachuting small radio devices into the walls of the low pressure eye, the men in the airplane receive news about the strength of the winds, and, according to their strength, classify the storm as a dangerous area, a tropical storm or, if the winds are over seventy-five m.p.h., a full-fledged hurricane.

The great storm system by now is moving, and its tremendously powerful winds combined with the constant heavy rain which accompanies it, are extremely dangerous. The satellites tell where the storm is, and captains of ships and pilots of airliners change course to avoid it. But for people on land, and on islands particularly, there is no getting out of the way. If the hurricane comes, it comes.

Thanks to the modern warning systems there is time to prepare, to haul small boats up, to shutter homes, and in many parts of the Caribbean, to move out of areas where there is likely to be flooding.

For Bermuda, isolated and far north of the usual spawning grounds, it is a time of watching and waiting. A moving hurricane can go anywhere, and about all a forecaster can say with absolute accuracy is that, for example, over the past six hours the storm has moved in a north-westerly direction at a speed of ten m.p.h. Perhaps five times out of ten the storm will continue moving in the same direction, and people who are north-west of the storm are wise if they take precautions.

There are however more predictable tracks which a number of hurricanes have followed, and it is probably fair to say that a hurricane which starts east of the Windwards/Leewards chain of the Caribbean and heads through or along the north side of the Bahamas chain, is more likely to come close to Bermuda than a hurricane starting elsewhere. What tends to happen as the storm moves westward along the Bahamas is that it starts a turning movement before it reaches the Gulf Stream. This turn takes the storm northwards, often toward the Bermuda ocean area, and Bermudians are faced with a monster heading for the island.

Whether it will hit Bermuda, or even brush the island with light gales, is unpredictable. What is likely to happen is that the great ocean waves produced by the hurricane, rolling way ahead of the storm itself, covering an enormous area of ocean, will probably boom and crash on the South Shore, making an exciting display but also making swimming dangerous.

Unlike areas further south, if sensible precautions are taken the heavy stone Bermuda house walls will normally withstand the worst the storm can fling, and the heavy roofs, although more vulnerable, are also good at standing up to the fury of the storm.

Eventually the storm passes north of Bermuda. When this happens it is likely to keep on going, usually dispersing as the water gets colder and the fuel for the great heat machine vanishes. Sometimes, however, it turns back, causing more worry for Bermudians. Sometimes it gets as far as Europe, causing damage as it smashes inland.

The hurricane is the most dramatic kind of weather Bermuda gets, but most of the time we are part of the general mid-Atlantic weather picture. In summer time the middle of the North Atlantic is dominated by a great area in which the atmosphere is heavier than the surrounding air, and this is called the Bermuda/Azores high.

The high helps Bermuda to have pleasant weather most of the summer, with south-westerly breezes and sunshine mixed with quick rainsqualls which can cause a heavy shower in one parish while a quarter of a mile down the road no rain falls at all.

In winter time the Bermuda/Azores high tends to move south, and the character of the weather changes. Cold air sweeps out from the American continent over the Atlantic, and, although warmed as it passes over the Gulf Stream, it brings colder temperatures to Bermuda. But the temperature never falls low enough to allow snow or ice—or almost never.

Ice in Bermuda

Occasionally flurries of very small snowflakes can be seen, which melt as they hit the ground, and even more rare is the formation of ice. The last time it was said to have occurred in Bermuda was in 1840, on Christmas Eve.

Said the *Royal Gazette* of the time: 'It will scarcely be credited—but such is the fact—that . . . *ice* was formed on the low ground, in the neighbourhood of the marshes in various parts of these islands, but more particularly in the parishes of Warwick, Paget, Pembroke and Devonshire. We are assured by gentlemen of unquestionable veracity that in many places it was a full quarter of an inch thick . . . Ice forming in Bermuda is almost without precedent; such a thing has not occurred within the recollection of our oldest inhabitants.'

Bermuda does get hail, causing great excitement as the little lumps of ice plummet from the skies.

During the winter the island can be hit by a series of storms caused by the passage of weather fronts across the Atlantic. These are started by masses of polar air moving south across Canada and the United States bringing blizzards to the continent. The fronts ride out across the Atlantic, and if the southern tail is long enough the storms sweep across Bermuda.

That is the time that passing ships get into trouble, either being damaged by the heavy winds or waves, or running short of fuel in battling the storm.

The Great Winter Shield

The great winter shield for Bermuda is the Gulf Stream. The stream is a great current in the ocean, fed by the Equatorial current and the warm water of the Caribbean and Gulf of Mexico, which starts off Florida and works its way north off the American coast, finally swinging across the top of the globe south of Greenland and Iceland to bring warm water and air to England, Norway, Finland and even Russia. It makes a big difference: Bermuda is on the same latitude as Savannah, Georgia, which has occasional snow and ice; Great Britain is on the same latitude as Labrador and Hudson Bay where the winter is long, the sea frozen and the snowfall enormous, while the sea rarely freezes off the coast of the British

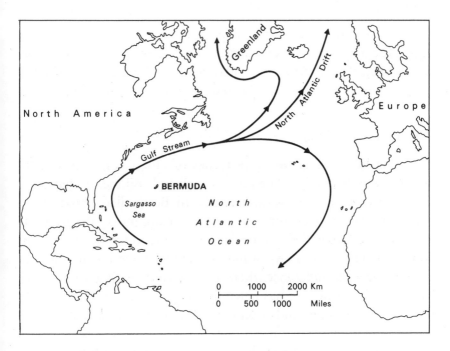

Mid-Atlantic sea currents.

Isles, the winters there are only about three months long and the snowfall occasional.

The other great oceanic fact which affects Bermuda is the Sargasso Sea, which is roughly the water equivalent of the Bermuda/Azores high. The Sargasso Sea is an ocean area in the centre of the great circle of currents sweeping the North Atlantic, and the floating Sargasso weed grows in the sea in great patches.

There were ancient tales that ships would be caught by the weed and be stuck in the Sargasso Sea for ever, and while these accounts are exaggerated, hulks have been found in the sea. Unfortunately today a proportion of the floating debris which has started to infest the Atlantic, principally oil, tar and plastic bottles, ends up in the Sargasso, and some of it winds up on Bermuda's shoreline.

The Sargasso weed also floats up on the island, but it is a welcome sight, for it has proved excellent as a fertilizer. In the past it was placed directly on the fields; today the best practice is considered to be to put it on a compost heap to rot down before using.

The Water Problem

Bermuda has an average of 58 inches of rain a year, and usually needs every drop of it. The porous rock and soil means that there are no rivers or streams, and nearly all Bermudian houses have their own tanks or cisterns to store water caught on the roofs. If there is little rainfall the water stored in the tanks begins to run low, and while nowadays water trucks and government supplies have made a big difference, there are still anxious times for householders when little rain has fallen for six or eight weeks.

In recent years Bermuda's underground water storage has proved to be bigger than anyone thought. It was always known that a shallow well dug near the shore would produce fresh water, and that this was floating on top of salt water. Much the same thing was known to be true around the marshes.

After 1950 it was gradually realized that this fresh water could also be obtained in the centre of the island, and that here the amount of fresh water was likely to be greater. It is now thought that salt water exists in the porous stone at sea level everywhere in Bermuda, and that the fresh water floating on top of it is shaped like a lens, with the thickest part underneath the centre of the land area, tapering away to the shoreline.

NOTE

Waterspouts　　Out on the great plains of the United States tornadoes, small, rapidly spinning circular storms, behaving like miniature but deadly hurricanes, can be very dangerous. Over the water

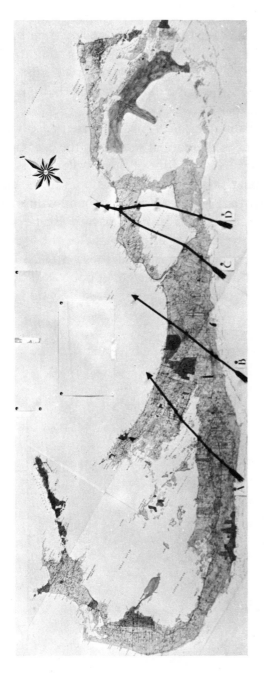

The routes of four tornadoes which stormed across Bermuda on Easter Sunday, 1953.

these same storms are called waterspouts, and on some muggy days, usually in July and August, they can be seen trying to form over the ocean—grey tails working their way down from the clouds toward the sea. When waterspouts hit land they become tornadoes, and leave a trail of damage.

What was probably Bermuda's worst experience with water-spouts occurred out of the normal season on the evening of Easter Day, 5th April 1953. At least four of them swept across the island, sounding like a buzz-saw and lifting trees up into the air. Several houses were destroyed; in one, at Crawl, a young woman was killed as the roof fell in. One taxi driver had a narrow escape on Harring-ton Sound Road; his cab was lifted by one of the tornadoes and deposited in the Sound. He managed to swim ashore. Another parked car was put overboard at the same spot.

Part 3

Story of the
Bermuda People

CHAPTER 6

Outline of Bermuda History

Christopher Carter was Bermuda's first settler, for he was the only member of the *Sea Venture*'s crew who stayed on in Bermuda until he died, a respected member of the island community. But the real settlement of Bermuda starts with the arrival of the ship *Plough* in 1612, bringing white settlers from England, and the return of the ship *Edwin* from the West Indies in 1616 with an Indian and a negro on board. Therefore, representatives of each of Bermuda's main races were already on the island by early in the seventeenth century.

What was to be the future of this small and isolated island? How was the community to survive? Bermuda might have developed into another Tristan da Cunha, an island group in the South Atlantic where a very small community existed right up to recent times on fish and potatoes and little else.

As it is, Bermuda has done better than that, and in our own time has reached a very high standard of living, with more than sufficient wealth flowing in to provide nearly everyone with the material comforts of life. But it has not always been so, and throughout the 400 years or so of Bermuda's history the problem of how the community is to make a living has been constant.

The smallness of the island has meant that during much of this time it was nearly impossible to grow enough food to feed the people. Bermuda had to find ways to pay for the food, clothing and comforts imported into the island. In more recent times this has been done by exploiting the island's advantages as a naval base and tourist centre—but at certain periods it was done by selling Bermudian produce abroad.

Tobacco

The first of these came soon after the early settlement of the island. People in Europe wanted tobacco, then a new discovery, and Bermuda, like Virginia, proved to have a good climate for growing it. In the early days this was the main way in which Bermudians earned money to purchase imports.

By the end of the seventeenth century however, Virginia had outstripped Bermuda in tobacco production, and the Bermuda people turned to new trades which kept the community going until after 1800.

Cedar, Salt and Sailors

The forest of Bermuda cedar was turned into ships; small fast sailing vessels, which roamed the Western Atlantic in time of peace carrying goods from one port to another. In time of war the owners of the ships would obtain letters-of-marque, official commissions which gave them the power to capture enemy vessels. Without a letter-of-marque such captures would have been piracy.

The sailors were the black and white Bermudian crews who sailed the ships, facing the hazards of the sea far from home. The salt was the salt of the Turks Islands, which are at the extreme eastern end of the Bahamas chain. The dry climate was ideal for making salt out of sea water, and the salt was carried to the West Indies, the settlements up and down the eastern seaboard of the United States, and the Grand Banks; it was essential for salting the fish which in turn was sold to the West Indian islands. The ships then loaded with food and other things needed in Bermuda and sailed back home.

The Koh-I-Noor—built at the end of the ship-building era.

With ships coming in from many parts of the Western Atlantic Bermudians learned a great deal about what was needed where, and struggled to supply these needs. Bermuda merchants were probably better informed than most of their West Indian and American rivals.

During the early nineteenth century these trades began to fail. The cedar was almost entirely used up; pictures of the island at the time show a landscape almost entirely without trees. Steam engines were being installed in ships, and after a slow start, by the middle of the century, steam-ships were regarded as reliable as sailing ships. The ships themselves were being built with iron ribs, and later entirely of iron or steel. Although some very fine vessels were built in Bermuda during the last century, as an industry shipbuilding was nearly dead. Bermudians continued to serve as sailors, but less and less frequently on Bermuda-owned vessels.

Down in the Turks Islands the century-long Bermuda dominance was taken away, and the group was placed under the Government of the Bahamas.

British Base

Fortunately for Bermudians the strategic importance of the island increased. After the American Revolutionary War the Royal Navy could no longer have naval bases on the American mainland, and Bermuda, situated halfway between the major British base at Halifax and the Bahamas, became increasingly important.

During the nineteenth century Great Britain and the United States were often on bad terms, and apart from the open war of 1812 there were several other moments when war seemed imminent. After every one of these alarms Britain improved the British base, until today there are massive Victorian fortifications in many places. Fortifications meant building, meant soldiers and sailors stationed here, and meant work for Bermuda.

The last spurt of fortification in Bermuda ended in the early years of this century, for even then the Royal Navy was returning to Europe to meet the threat posed by the new fleet being built by Kaiser Wilhelm II of Germany.

In any case, by then relationships between Britain and the United States were generally good, and in 1917 were cemented further when the United States entered the First World War on the side of Britain and France. Between the wars the good relations continued, and gradually the great British base here died, until today its remnants are a few officers and men stationed at the former Dockyard on Ireland Island. They support a squadron which generally consists of only two frigates.

Potatoes and Onions

During the nineteenth century also Bermudians revived agriculture and developed an excellent market in the northern United States in spring vegetables. The Agricultural Exhibition started at this time and farmers competed with one another, as people still do today, keeping alive the feeling many Bermudians have for working the soil, growing their own vegetables and flowers.

A number of events brought the agricultural period to an end. The discovery of how to refrigerate railroad boxcars meant that farmers in the southern United States could send their spring vegetables to New York and other cities which had formerly purchased from Bermuda, and at the same time increasingly harsh American customs duties on imported food pushed up the price of Bermuda vegetables. Gradually farming died, until now the few remaining cultivated fields grow crops entirely for Bermuda's own consumption.

Tourist Trade

Even as the British base was being improved in the early years of the twentieth century, another industry was rising. In the late nineteenth century people had come to believe that plenty of sunshine was good for the human body, and continued improvements in steam-ships meant that Americans could come here easily during the hard winter to refresh themselves in the warmth of Bermuda's climate. Hotels were built, and these provided work and income for the islanders.

HAMILTON HOTEL

MERICAN HOUSE & CHURCH STREET.

PRINCESS HOTEL

Views of Hamilton at the end of the 19th century.

It was a trend which was carefully nurtured and developed, until today most Bermudians live in one way or another on the proceeds of the tourist business. Catering to tourists is reckoned by many people to bring in a large proportion of the community's overall income.

American Bases

Another important development came during the Second World War, when the United States, fearing that Britain might be overwhelmed by Hitler's Germany, obtained the right to build bases on Bermuda. These compensated for the economic loss resulting from the slow British withdrawal, and they still play an important part in Bermuda life.

Exempted Companies

The most recent economic change has been the discovery, principally by British, American and Canadian companies, that Bermuda is a good place from which to operate. At first the main reason was heavy taxation in the home countries, but other considerations such as complicated laws governing company operations in other places, have also been important.

The growth of this business in Bermuda has resulted in increasing numbers of jobs being available in clerical fields requiring skills in shorthand, typing and accounting, and today Bermudians are becoming increasingly skilled in this kind of work.

For over twenty years an effort was made to develop light industries at the former Dockyard, without a great deal of success. But throughout the island there are an increasing number of small industries making goods to sell to visitors and Bermudians, and the community may be heading toward an era when Bermuda-made goods, like the ships of the past, play an important part in the economy.

The life of Bermudians has been constantly governed by these economic factors, and our skills and folk memories look back to the things our forefathers had to do to stay alive. In the future, as the world turns on through the centuries ahead, we may have to learn new ways to help keep this small and isolated community going.

This chapter is an outline of Bermuda history, of the story to be told in the following pages. The story starts where chapter 3 ended; with the adventures of the three men left on Bermuda when the *Patience* set sail for England.

NOTE

The Bounty of the Deep   Fishing and whaling were never vital to Bermuda's economy, but both were important to individuals. Fishing, particularly, has been a sport and a business throughout Bermuda's story; whaling started in the seventeenth century and was only discontinued in the early years of this century.

Whaling was an exciting and dangerous business. When the whale's spout was seen, boats would be manned and the chase would start. When the boat was close enough the harpooner threw his harpoon into the whale, which usually reacted wildly, diving deep or swimming at great speed. Eventually, however, the whale tired and then the whalers could attack it with lances. Eventually it was pulled to shore, the fatty blubber cut off and cooked in large iron pots until it turned to oil. The whale meat was eaten, and the bone used for a variety of purposes.

The most famous Bermuda story about whaling occurred in this century. In St David's, according to the story, a number of people had doubts about the Bible story of the prophet Jonah being swallowed by a whale and later being coughed up. The whale's stomach, they said, was too small. Mr Tommy Fox, a notable

This reconstruction shows the dangers of whaling.

personality on the island, said the doubters were wrong, and the next time a whale was caught he crawled down into the stomach. He declared that it was a 'considerable apartment'.

Sport fishing as opposed to fishing for food has become a highly developed pastime in the past fifty years as motorboats have been more widely used. Today the fishing guides compete in importance with the men who pull their fishpots every day and sell their catch to hotels, restaurants and the general public.

Bermuda received a large addition to the area under its control when, through international treaties, it gained exclusive fishing rights to a vast circle of ocean, stretching 200 miles—a third of the distance to Cape Hatteras—from its shores. Bermuda's territorial waters also increased from three miles offshore to twelve miles. These changes stimulated fresh interest in commercial fishing and spurred the Government to purchase a fisheries research vessel.

CHAPTER 7

The First Settlers

One day Edward Chard was walking along the seashore. He and Christopher Carter and Robert Waters were now alone on the island. Matthew Somers had sailed away in the *Patience*, and the three of them, at the suggestion of Carter, had agreed to stay behind. They must have thought that another ship would come to Bermuda soon, but in fact two long, lonely years stretched ahead of them.

Chard was looking for anything he could pick up that might be useful—and then he spotted a large lump of a grey, waxy substance. Having some knowledge of the sea and its curiosities, he went over to it, and as he thought, it was ambergris.

Ambergris was then, and still is, in some processes, a major ingredient in making perfume. It comes from sick whales and was and is very rare. In the coinage of the early seventeenth century it was worth three English pounds an ounce in London, and so even a small piece was a considerable treasure.

The lump found by Chard weighed eighty pounds, and there were other small lumps beside. He ran to tell Carter and Waters, and the three of them heaved the ambergris away from the shore and into a hiding place.

Until now the three men had lived happily with each other, but the ambergris changed that. Chard and Waters, particularly, each longed to have sole possession of the treasure, and the silent hills re-echoed to the noise of their threats and quarrels. Carter, who was an easy-going man, hid all the weapons, because he was very much afraid of being left alone on Bermuda.

Time, and the solitude and peace of the island, gradually worked on Chard and Waters, and they saw the stupidity of their behaviour. They patched up a peace between them, and then all three, at Waters' suggestion, started work on a boat to take them to Virginia or Newfoundland; but before they had made much progress a ship entered St George's Harbour.

Arrival of English Settlers

It was the *Plough*, and aboard were fifty settlers and the first Governor, Richard Moore. The ship anchored off an island which they called Smith's Island in honour of Sir Thomas Smith, one of the principal shareholders of the Virginia Company.

The three men came to them, and shortly afterwards the company moved over to the larger island which they called St George's, partly in honour of the patron saint of England, and partly in honour of Sir George Somers.

Governor Moore questioned Chard about any discoveries the three men had made, but Chard kept quiet about the ambergris. Soon afterwards he and Waters and Carter tried to bargain with the skipper of the *Plough*, Captain Davis, to take the ambergris to England privately.

Carter mulled the matter over in his mind; and decided to tell Moore. The Governor seized the ambergris, imprisoned Chard, reproved the others in the plot, and decided to send the ambergris to England, a portion at a time, so that the Virginia Company would not lose interest in the new colony. Chard and Waters eventually emigrated to Virginia, for Chard was released after Moore left, but Carter stayed in Bermuda for the rest of his life. He was offered St David's Island as a reward for revealing the plot, but

Hog money—the first coinage sent to Bermuda. The design commemorates the hogs found by the 'Sea Venture' company.

picked Cooper's Island (now part of the U.S. Naval Air Station) instead. He thought treasure was buried there, but never found any.

Defence of Bermuda

Rumours that the Spaniards disliked the English settling in Bermuda and were thinking of taking it for themselves had been current in England when the *Plough* sailed, and Governor Moore quickly occupied the settlers with building fortifications. He was a carpenter by trade, and an able one, and the forts went up quickly.

The rumours in London were true; in the council chambers of Madrid the King of Spain and his advisers considered plan after plan for capturing Bermuda, for even though there was peace between England and Spain in Europe, there was not much peace in the Western Atlantic. The Spaniards did not like the idea of Bermuda being in English hands because Spanish ships passed close by on their way home, when they were laden with the wealth of the Caribbean. Fortunately for Moore and the settlers the King and his council could never make up their minds, but in 1614 Captain Domingo de Ulivari, bound for Spain in company with another ship, decided to do a little spying.

The ships sailed in toward Castle Harbour, but smoke signals gave the alarm to the Governor, and he hurried over to his newly-built fort at Castle Island, ready for the emergency which he had foreseen.

Moore and the garrison only had one cannon which was working. The Governor carefully sighted the cannon and fired it. The round cannon-ball went over the mast of the leading ship. Hastily reloading the gun, the Governor took aim again, and this time succeeded in sending a ball whistling through the ship's rigging.

It was enough. The Spanish, who were handicapped by having to have a boat out ahead checking whether the channel was deep enough, turned about and set out to sea. The Governor and his men breathed a sigh of relief. They only had one cannon-ball left.

Governor Moore under Attack

Hard as the Governor laboured—there is reason to think that he even made the handsome table which serves as an altar at St Peter's Church—the settlers were by no means content, and sent adverse reports about him back to London.

By this time a number of shareholders of the Virginia Company had purchased Bermuda for £2,000, and the island was now under the control of the Bermuda or Somers Island Company. The shareholders of the new company were unhappy because no more ambergris had been found, and there was no abundance of pearls; in short they had paid out money and received little in return. The blame was falling on the Governor's shoulders, so Moore decided to return to Britain to defend himself.

A reconstruction of Governor Moore's defence against the Spaniards.

He left Bermuda in the control of six men, each one of whom was to be Governor for a month. It is known as the time of the Six Governors, and it was an odd period, with one man setting the island by the ears, another leaving on a piratical expedition, and others, like Christopher Carter, taking it easy and letting others do so too. It is said of Carter's month: 'Not a hoe, axe, pickaxe or shovel was so much as once heard in the streets, nor an oar seen or heard unless when their stout stomachs compelled them to it.'

Governor Daniel Tucker

Word eventually reached London, and the company decided to send out someone who could do something about the situation. They picked Daniel Tucker, who owned a plantation in Virginia, and had a reputation of being a strong man.

His reputation was well-deserved. Governor Tucker, who is still celebrated in the United States in the folk-song 'Ole Dan Tucker', quickly changed the 'perpetual Christmas' which reports to London had spoken about. He did not hesitate to use the lash to enforce his commandments, one man even being hanged for talking against him, and soon the settlers were hard at work, if not happily.

One group, led by Richard Sanders, suggested they should build a good-sized boat for the Governor to fish in, no matter how bad the weather. The Governor agreed to what he thought was a kind offer, the men cleared off to a distant part of the island, and built the boat. When Governor Tucker went to fetch it he found the men had sailed away in it. After a long and hazardous voyage the runaways finally made a landfall at Ireland, 3,500 miles away.

Governor Tucker sailed to Bermuda on a ship called the *George* which was accompanied by another, called the *Edwin*. The Edwin was sent to the West Indies and in 1616, soon after the Sanders group had stolen away, she returned to Bermuda.

Aboard her were two men who became Bermuda's first black and Indian settlers. Their names are not recorded, but they were not necessarily slaves. The Somers Island Company had authorised Governor Tucker to import black people as divers, and during a trial of this period a black man was sentenced to become a slave during the Governor's pleasure. His name, the first black person's name to be recorded, was given as Symon the Negro.

One of Governor Tucker's biggest problems was an invasion of rats. Back in 1614 they had landed from a ship which brought meal, and by 1616 they had infested most of Bermuda. It was a plague which neither dogs, cats nor traps seemed able to combat, but soon after Governor Tucker left many of the rats disappeared during a particularly severe winter.

Burnt House Hill in Warwick is supposed to be named after this period, for an attempt was made to kill off the rats, some of which nested in trees, by burning great sections of land, and Burnt House Hill is possibly one of the areas burnt.

Norwood's Survey

During Tucker's administration Bermuda was first properly surveyed by a remarkable man named Richard Norwood. Norwood, using a crude diving device, had salvaged the guns from a sunken ship in England, and the Somers Island Company directors thought that he would be able to find pearls in Bermuda. Instead, Norwood found himself put to work as a surveyor, a job he was well qualified to do. His map remains remarkably accurate, and has stood the test of time right up to the present. It was he who divided Bermuda into eight tribes (now parishes) and 'the public land' at St George's.

He made one mistake in dividing the land, ending up with a surplus between Southampton and Sandys. This became known as the Overplus (today there is still an Overplus Lane) and the Governor grabbed it as a personal reward for himself.

Tucker had many enemies in Bermuda by now, and this last move led several of them to complain to London. Some months afterwards Governor Tucker was advised to return to London to defend himself, which he did, opening the way for one of Bermuda's finest Governors, Nathaniel Butler.

In London Tucker was reproved for his land grab, but allowed to keep a portion of the Overplus, and later he returned to Bermuda to live.

NOTES

(a) The adventures of Richard Sanders were not over when he arrived in Ireland. He soon afterwards set sail for the East Indies, where he happened to buy a locked chest for three or four shillings. No key could be found and Sanders was sorry he had spent the money. One day having nothing else to do, he forced the lock—and found £1,000.

(b) *Bermuda Names*   Names of a number of the earliest settlers who arrived here during the first fifteen years still crop up in Bermuda today, either as family names or place names. Here are some of them. Spellings may have changed somewhat over the passage of time.

Abbott, Adams, Allen, Amorie, Atwood.

Baker, Ball, Barrett, Bassett, Beake, Bell, Bosse, Bostock, Brangman, Browne, Burgess, Burrows.

Cann, Carter, Chamberlain, Clarke, Cooke, Cooper, Cox.

Davis, Deane, Dunscombe.

Edmunds, Ely, Evans.

Ffludd, Foord, Frith.

Green, Guin (later Gwynne?).

Hall, Harford, Harman, Harriott, Harris, Harrison, Harvey, Hayward, Higgs, Hill, Hinson, Hughes.

Joel, Johnson, Jones.

Kempthorne.

Lambert, Lea, Lewis, Llewellyn, Lucroft (later Leycroft?), Lunne.

Middleton, Miller, Milles, Milner, Mitchell, Morgan, Morris.
Nash, Newman, Norwood.
Outerbridge.
Palmer, Parker, Paynter, Peniston, Perinchief, Pitman, Pitt, Plaice, Powell.
Reynor, Richardson, Roberts, Robinson.
Scott, Scroggan, Seymour, Sears, Smith, Stafford, Stevens, Stokes, Stowes, Symonds, Swan.
Tatem, Trimingham, Trott, Tucker.
Vaughn.
Walker, Warde, Washington, Watlington, Webb, Welch, Welman, West, Wilkinson, Williams, Wilson, Wiseman, Wood.
Younge.

CHAPTER 8

The Company's Great Gift

The Bermuda Company was a cause of great pain and trouble to many of the early settlers. The company attempted to give instructions from London about small details of life in the island; it tried to keep all the trade going in and out of Bermuda in its own hands; its very existence prolonged island quarrels.

The company gave one great gift to Bermuda which was a parliament. It was not exactly like the Legislature we know today, and its powers were more limited, but at its meetings representatives of the settlers could put their point of view and know that they would have a hearing.

It was a parliament which gave trouble to Governors and to the British Government; it was often slow in its workings, but it endured and gave the Bermuda people a representative institution throughout the long history of the island. Bermudians gained a great deal from it, and it helped bring the island through many difficult times. Today the parliament is stronger than ever before, but how this came about is left for a later chapter.

Governor Nathaniel Butler

The Parliament ordered by the Company was instituted by Governor Nathaniel Butler, who succeeded Governor Tucker. Butler stands out among Governors not just because he instituted Parliament, but also because of his intelligence, ability and energy; qualities which he was going to need in Bermuda.

He faced a crisis the very day he arrived. The new Governor arrived aboard the ship *Warwick* and the acting Governor, Miles Kendall, came out to greet him. Butler invited Kendall, his councillors and the island's only clergyman, the Rev Lewis Hughes, to dinner on the ship, which was anchored in Castle Harbour not far from Castle Island. Suddenly flames burst from the Castle, and everyone was forced to hurry ashore to fight the fire, which did a great deal of damage.

So one of Butler's first jobs was to repair the Castle. Then further problems developed when a tremendous hurricane hit Bermuda, damaging many houses and sinking the *Warwick*.

The problem of finding arms Governor Butler solved by raising guns from the *Warwick* and later from the *Sea Venture*, for the old ship's hull had not yet been torn apart by the fierce underwater surge.

The Governor waited until the new St Peter's Church had been completed before he summoned representatives to meet there for the first Parliament. It was a momentous occasion, and Governor Butler gave a superb speech, parts of which hold good to this day.

Thanks be to God, that we are thus met, to so good an end as the making of good and wholesome laws; and I hope the blessed effect will manifest that this course was inspired from heaven into the hearts of the undertakers in England [shareholders of the Bermuda Company], to pronounce and offer it unto us, for the singular good and welfare of this plantation . . .

Take due notice that we come not hither for ourselves only, and to serve our turns, or any man else's in particular, but to serve and regard the public. We are, therefore, to rid ourselves of all base desires of gain; we are to despise all private interests, thus far at least, as to cause them to give way to the general.

It may well be that some men chosen to be burgesses[members of the House of Assembly] here may find some bills preferred into this Assembly that may strike at some getting and income of theirs in particular. If they do so, let them remember their oaths, let them not shame themselves, and the place they hold here . . . If, in their own consciences, they find that hitherto they have done injury to a common good, let them not augment it by obstinacy . . . I grant there is a freedom of speech and opinion with modesty to be held by every man here . . .

Let us beseech God to inspire us with peaceable spirits, and such thoughts and desires as become honest, loyal and wise men, such as may be for his glory and the forming of this hopeful and forward plantation. . . .

Although the first meeting of the House of Assembly was held in St Peter's Church, Governor Butler also intended to build a house where Parliament could meet and where the courts could be held. In doing so he created a building which in many ways gave a lead to the traditional Bermuda house. The building, considerably altered through the years, has survived to the present day. Recently, principally through the interest of Mr Hereward Watlington, Dr Henry Wilkinson, Mr Hinson Cooper and Sir John Cox, the State House in St George's has been restored according to Governor Butler's plan.

When the building was completed is not known, but presumably it was finished before October 1622, when Nathaniel Butler sailed for Virginia to inspect that colony before he returned to England.

The Civil War

There were troubles in the colonies, but worse trouble was brewing at home. Varying religious beliefs were at the root of much of the discord. The Protestant Reformation in Europe had ended the complete power of the Roman Catholic Church, and had led to the development of many new ideas about how God wished people to worship. The supporters of each idea believed that their way of worshipping God was the right and true way, and that it was their Christian duty to oppose, even in battle, those who supported different methods of worship. Seventeenth-century Europe was therefore the scene of several religious wars.

Britain was also affected by the clash of religious ideas. The country had become officially Protestant in the sixteenth century, when the Church of England was set up. There still were Roman Catholics, but they were regarded with great suspicion by most of the population. Some of the more extreme Protestants became known as Puritans, who, as their name suggests, wanted the worship of God to be as pure and simple as possible. Queen Elizabeth I managed to keep an uneasy peace between the religious groups, giving the Church of England her own support. Her successor, King James I, who was not such a strong ruler, found it much more difficult to control the religious quarrels.

The situation worsened even further when his son, King Charles I married a Roman Catholic, showed himself sympathetic towards Roman Catholics, and appointed a man of similar views, William Laud, as Archbishop of Canterbury (the most important position in the Church of England). Archbishop Laud not only tried to make the services of the Church of England more elaborate but he also started a campaign against the Puritans, fining or imprisoning them. Many of them therefore escaped across the Atlantic to start the colonies in New England where they could worship as they wished.

However King Charles still had plenty of enemies left in England. There were many who disliked his religious views, and who bitterly opposed the way he ruled the country in general. This discontent was expressed by Parliament, and the situation eventually grew so bad that a civil war started with the King and his supporters on one side, and Parliament and its supporters on the other. The war finally ended with the defeat and execution of the King.

A reconstruction of a ducking-stool being used to punish an erring wife at the time of the Independents.

In Bermuda the Puritans, known as Independents, were very powerful. Many of them had left England to escape persecution but their rule in Bermuda was oppressive and intolerant. One of those who suffered from their intolerance was Richard Norwood who had returned to Bermuda as schoolmaster in 1638. He spoke out against the Independents and as a result was forced out of his job.

In 1646 Governor Josias Forster (whose chair is now the throne chair in the Legislative Council chamber) allowed the Puritan ministers to have the upper hand because he was powerless to do otherwise, but he was soon replaced from London by Governor Thomas Turner. Turner called a meeting of the House of Assembly, which turned out to be entirely anti-puritan. The Assembly forbade the holding of Puritan services, and the Independents complained to London. Throughout the period of the Civil War London, where the headquarters of the Bermuda Company was situated, was dominated by Parliamentary forces. In response to the Puritans' complaints the Company sent out an instruction that Norwood should be Governor, assisted by William Wilkinson (a Puritan) and Captain Christopher Leacraft who, unknown to the Company, was dead.

There was an immediate uproar, for despite his clash with them Norwood was felt to be too friendly to the Independents, and a demonstration at St Peter's Church prevented him from reading himself in as Governor. Norwood was not anxious for a fight, so he declined to serve, and the people of Bermuda would not accept Wilkinson as Governor.

Faced with this situation the Council in Bermuda restored Governor Turner, but some months later the news was received that King Charles had been executed in London. This news horrified most of the settlers, and soon the anti-puritans called out the militia. The militia, headed by John Trimingham, called themselves 'The Army', and marched on St George's. There they ensured that Governor Turner and his Council declared their allegiance to the Prince of Wales, the future King Charles II, and then they put

Turner out of office and replaced him with Trimingham. It was a miniature civil war.

The anti-puritans tried to persuade the Independents to leave Bermuda, and some of them went to the Bahamas and others went to other West Indian islands. There are still surnames in the Bahamas which are the same as those held by Bermudians.

The following year the Company in London, more confident of its authority now that England was unified under the power of Oliver Cromwell, replaced Trimingham with Josias Forster again, and the civil war, the only one in Bermuda's history, was over.

Things ran more quietly in Bermuda during the remainder of Cromwell's period of rule, known as the Commonwealth, but when King Charles II was restored to the throne in 1660, Bermudians were quick to give him allegiance.

Norwood's Second Survey

After the Restoration Norwood started his second survey of Bermuda, and it is on this survey that the land-holdings in Bermuda were based. Norwood's method of running his property dividing lines straight across the island from the South Shore to the North Shore still leaves its mark on Bermuda. There are old stone walls which march in straight lines up and down hill, and aerial photographs of Bermuda show even more clearly this north-south alignment.

The map made from Norwood's Survey—the land was divided into shares for the Bermuda Company shareholders. This map was used to determine land boundaries nearly up to modern times.

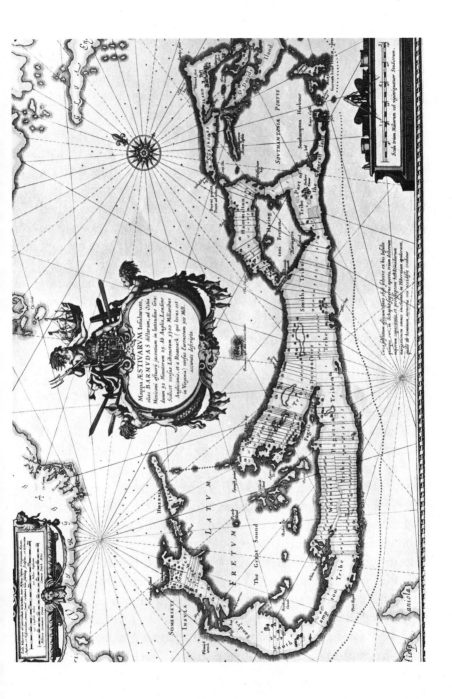

NOTE

Other Achievements of Governor Butler   In Bermuda Governor Butler is remembered mainly as an able administrator, but he was also a writer and warrior. After leaving Bermuda he went to Virginia on behalf of the Earl of Warwick to make a report on that colony, which had just suffered an Indian uprising in which large numbers of settlers had been killed. While in Virginia he took part in a campaign against the Indians, and then he returned to England where he wrote a book about the Indian massacre called *The Unmasking of Virginia*. The Virginia Company was already in trouble, and this book helped to bring about its downfall, which finally occurred in 1624, two years after the massacre.

He probably also wrote a book about Bermuda at the same time, but it was not published until 1882 when the manuscript, owned by the British Museum, was re-discovered by Governor Lefroy. The name of the author is not given with the manuscript, but Nathaniel Butler seems the most likely person.

Soon afterwards Governor Butler commanded a ship in an expedition which tried to capture the Isle of Ré off the port of La Rochelle on the Bay of Biscay coast of France.

Then he undertook a more exciting job. In 1630 a group of Puritans, anxious to harm Spain, decided to settle on an island deep in the Caribbean off the coast of what is now Nicaragua, right in the centre of the Spanish possessions. At first the settlement, known as Providence Island, was run on peaceful lines, but in the late 1630s the Spanish attacked. They were defeated, but the Providence Adventurers in London decided they would take strong measures. The most important of these was the appointment of Butler as Governor.

Butler quickly gathered a fleet of English and Dutch privateers and attacked the town of Truxillo, gaining 16,000 pieces of eight (Spanish dollars) from it. Butler sailed back to England with the loot, but after he had gone the enraged Spanish attacked Providence, failed to capture it, tried again and in May 1641, succeeded.

CHAPTER 9

Salt and Pirates

In the year 1684, in a courtroom in London, it was decided that the Bermuda Company should be dissolved. Efforts to save the Company had been going on for some time, but they were in vain.

At the start the Bermuda Company had been made up of a number of distinguished and able men, and Bermuda was one of the few colonial possessions of England. But by 1684 the tremendous movement of people across the Atlantic Ocean, the establishment of the great New England colonies, and the capture of Jamaica and New Amsterdam (renamed New York) had made Bermuda seem less and less important.

The Bermuda tobacco crop was uncertain and could not compete with the crop produced in Virginia where thousands of acres were under cultivation. As Bermuda faded in importance so the calibre of the men associated with it became less impressive too, and with the judge's decision, Bermuda was now a royal colony. This meant that it was governed directly by the British Government. The Bermudians were delighted to be free of the Company's restrictive rule.

Since the production of tobacco had been so disappointing the time had come to change the economic basis of the island. The sea was calling, the cedar was waiting to be turned into ships, and down to the south there was an important and valuable crop to be gathered: salt.

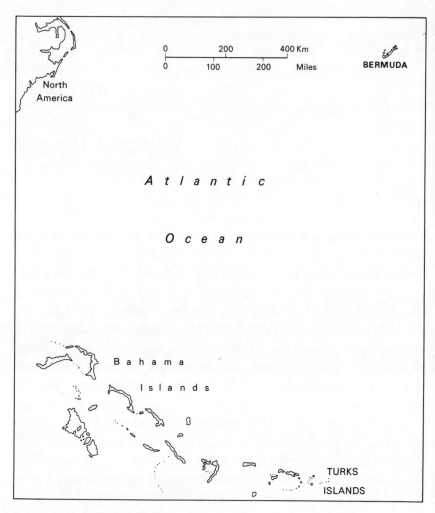

Bermuda and the Turks Islands.

The Salt Trade

It was in 1678 that Bermudians first sailed south to the Turks Islands, six years before the end of the company. They soon realized the possibilities of trading in salt; it was a precious commodity in days when fish and meat could only be preserved by using it. For fourteen years they made salt in peace, pumping water into settling ponds, waiting for the sun to evaporate the water, and raking up the salt. In 1692 however, they faced a new and more energetic Governor in the Bahamas; he was actually a Bermudian named Nicholas Trott, whose family had played a major role in bringing the Bermuda Company to an end. Under orders from the English courtiers who at that point owned the Bahamas, he started levying taxes on salt exports from the Turks Islands. The Bermudians who thought the Bahamas had no right to do this, protested bitterly in London, but things became even worse in the early eighteenth century when Bermuda ships were seized by the new Governor of the Bahamas, Elias Haskett, and sold. It was Haskett who once said he had never hanged a Bermudian, 'but would make no more to do it than to hang a dog'.

Not surprisingly, there was almost war between Bermuda and the Bahamas. Haskett and his friends were racketeers, almost pirates, and in Bermuda Governor Benjamin Bennett gave Bermudians letters-of-marque so that they could attack such pirates legally.

But worse was to come. In Europe Britain, Holland and Austria were fighting France and some factions in Spain over the question of who should be the King of Spain. In Bermuda this meant keeping men at home in case of invasion, rather than letting them sail away. The Turks Islands however were exposed to attack and in 1706 were captured by the French and Spanish. In 1710 however, Captain Lewis Middleton and a crew of Bermudians went south in the Bermuda privateer *Rose* and recaptured the Turks. This time there was no interference from the Bahamas, because the French and Spanish had almost wiped out the settlement there.

Peace in Europe came in 1713, but there was little peace on the sea. This time it was declared pirates who grabbed the rest of the Bahamas chain and threatened the Bermudians. What were they to do? Governor Bennett decided to try peaceful means, and sent his

The pirate Blackbeard who terrorised the Caribbean.

son John south to issue pardons to all who surrendered. The trip was a failure, and now Bermuda itself was in real danger. Rumours came that the notorious pirates Blackbeard (whose real name was

Edward Teach) and Major Stede Bonnet were considering an attack on the island, which would have made an ideal pirate base, and once more the Bermuda militia were put on guard and men were kept home to garrison the forts.

This was the height of pirate power in these waters, and soon the tide turned. A strong man who had been a privateer himself, Woodes Rogers, took over the Bahamas and ended the pirate rule.

Bermudian Sailors

The crews of Bermuda ships were composed of black and white men, and their adventures were by no means confined to salt raking. Governor John Hope has told us what generally went on during the eighteenth century. The small, fast ships would slip out through the Bermuda reefs and head first for the Turks Islands. There the skippers would land their white crews, who would stay in Turks for up to a year, while the captains and the black sailors ventured further south 'a marooning' as Governor Hope put it. This meant 'fishing for turtle, diving upon wrecks and sometimes trading with pirates'.

If they were lucky in their marooning they sailed to Curaçao or St Eustatius or St Thomas or to the French Islands 'where they are always well receiv'd without any questions asked' and sold the cargo—and sometimes the ship too. If the ship was not sold they went back to Turks, picked up the salt cargo and the rest of the crew, and went off to North America to sell the salt before coming home to Bermuda.

The men had an adventurous and exciting time, always with the chance that they would come home rich men, but in many ways life was tougher for the women. They were left at home, and when the white sails of the ship dipped over the horizon there was no saying when they would see their menfolk again, if ever. There are many sad tales told about those seafaring days, but there are also happier ones.

The Story of Captain Lewis

One sad tale tells of the encounter in 1692 of several Bermuda ships with Captain John Lewis, of whom it is written 'this worthy gentleman was early a pirate'. Lewis became a pirate captain when he ran away from Havana with six companions in a canoe, and surprised a small Spanish vessel. He captured several more ships and gathered about forty followers.

From one of the captured ships he learned that a fine Bermuda-built ten-gun brigantine under the command of a Captain Tucker lay in the Bay of Campeachy, on the Mexican coast. Lewis decided to have her, and offered Tucker 10,000 pieces of eight. Tucker refused to sell, and called together the captains of ten other small Bermuda vessels nearby. He suggested that each let him have some men, and he would fight Lewis, in an attempt to keep them all safe. The captains refused but they did agree to set sail immediately.

Then the wind failed, but Lewis came in chase, using oars. Once more Tucker signalled to the Bermuda sloops, urging them to send men aboard, but once again they refused. The wind came up again, and Captain Tucker trimmed his sails, let loose a broadside into the pirate ship, and escaped. Captain Joseph Dill on one of the sloops fired two guns into the pirate, but then one of his cannon burst, killing three men. The other captains tamely surrendered.

Lewis went from one ship to another, stealing cargo and money. He also either persuaded or forced forty black sailors and one white carpenter into his service, and took the biggest sloop for his piratical adventures.

It must have been a sad day in Bermuda when the other vessels came back with fortunes gone and loved ones missing. Some of the lost sailors may have made their way home later, for a number of men managed to escape from Lewis, but there were others used to a life of slavery who probably welcomed freedom, even if it meant being a pirate.

Some pirates were utterly inhuman. The tale is told of the capture of a Bermuda vessel commanded by another Nicholas Trott in 1722. The pirate captain, Spriggs, a New Englander, found little loot so he let his men pull the Bermudians up into the rigging, one after another, and for the fun of it let them drop down to bounce on the deck. Those that survived were freed, many of them crippled for life.

Thomas Tew's Voyage

On a happier note, a number of Bermudians took part in one highly successful piratical voyage. The story starts in 1691 when Thomas Tew, a seaman from Rhode Island, arrived in Bermuda. Tew had some money and bought a share in the sloop *Amity* and obtained a letter-of-marque from the Governor; he was given the job of capturing a French trading post on the River Gambia in Africa.

He sailed from Bermuda in company with another vessel but soon a storm separated the ships and Tew suggested to his crew that he knew a way to make them rich forever. 'A gold chain or a wooden leg! We'll stand by you!' the crew is reported to have said, and Tew headed around the Cape of Good Hope and up the East African coast toward the Red Sea. Their luck was good; they fell in with a large and richly laden Arabian vessel carrying 300 soldiers and much gold. The Bermudians attacked, swarming aboard the larger ship, the Arabians turned out to be cowardly, and the ship was captured. Each man's share of the booty was £3,000.

They then set sail for Madagascar, which was then a pirate stronghold, and soon afterwards fell in with Captain Mission, a famous French pirate. Mission had already created a settlement, which he called Libertatia, where there were no slaves and black and white mingled in equality. Tew made several more voyages with the pirates, but eventually chose to go back to America. He left a number of his original crew behind who preferred to live in Madagascar and took aboard those who wished to return to their homes in the American colonies.

Tew landed with £80,000 in booty, and his personal share was said to be £12,000. The original owners of the *Amity* were paid their shares, and became wealthy men.

The Treasure Reef

That adventure was thoroughly unusual, but there was another in which Bermudians raked in a good deal of money, only to be forced to disgorge most of it later.

Down in the Bahamas there is a reef known as the Ambrosias reef, and this was the scene of a terrible shipwreck of a Spanish treasure galleon. Some of the treasure was taken from the ship and left on the reef to be picked up later, but the reef grew, covering the gold.

Eventually news about the treasure reached the ears of the Duke of Albemarle, son of one of Cromwell's generals. The Duke raised £800 and sent out a two-ship expedition under the command of Captain William Phipps, a New Englander.

At first the expedition had no luck, but just as they were despairing of ever finding the treasure an Indian diver brought up a pretty seaflower. Stuck to the bottom was a coin. The treasure was found; but food and water were running out. Phipps was forced to sail away to get supplies, but despite all his care, news of the treasure quickly got about, and when he returned to the reef he found a number of Bermudian and New England vessels crowded around, the crews all busy diving for gold and silver.

Phipps chased them away, but he still managed to find plenty to load onto his ships. Nevertheless, he also forced the Bermudians to give up their share, and the old records tell of Spanish money which was taken away from Bermuda and shipped to England.

One Bermudian played a particularly important role in this salvage venture. He invented a diving bell which was used by Phipps' divers.

The Bermuda Rig

It was about this time that the Bermuda sail came into sufficient prominence to be recognized as a special rig. A triangular sail, in those days it was loose-footed without a boom. Bermudians found that it was excellent in making a sailboat work its way against the wind, but only since the First World War has it been accepted by yachtsmen as the best small boat sail.

The rig is similar to a Dutch rig of the time, and may have been introduced to Bermuda by a Dutch shipwright who was saved from

A Bermuda trading sloop—part of a crude picture of
St George's waterfront, probably made by a sailor.

a shipwreck and took employment here under Governor Nathaniel Butler. The rig lasted in Bermuda for three centuries before receiving world-wide adoption. Its final home-grown form is the rig still used in Bermuda sailing dinghies.

NOTE

The Militia   During most of Bermuda's history Bermudians have taken some of the responsibility for the island's defence. Governor Moore and the first settlers manned the gun at Castle Island and drove off the Spanish vessels. In a different role as we have seen, 'The Army' proclaimed allegiance to King Charles II and made John Trimingham Governor, which shows the power which the militia had at the time.

Some of the small militia forts can still be seen. There is one near the Martello Tower at Ferry Reach, and another at the east end of Church Bay. Gates Fort, St George's, is a reconstruction of an important militia fort and battery.

Records show that the militia included members of both races, even when most black people were slaves. During Governor Bennett's time 600 slaves were provided with lances and drilled, but during the same administration the number of white sailors on outward-bound Bermuda vessels was reduced to keep more white men on the island.

The militia tended to fade away in times of peace during the eighteenth century, but would be whipped into shape again when war threatened. They were also called on when a slave rising seemed possible in 1761.

During the nineteenth century the militia disappeared. It was finally revived in a different form when the Bermuda Militia Artillery and the Bermuda Volunteer Rifle Corps were formed in the 1890s: The units underwent various changes, finally joining and becoming the Bermuda Regiment in the 1960s.

Jokes were often made about the militia of the eighteenth century, but without them and the cannon they manned Bermuda would have seemed an easy prey to pirates or enemy warships. Bermuda's amateur soldiers played an important role in keeping Bermuda under one flag throughout her history.

CHAPTER 10

Slavery in Bermuda

Slavery in Bermuda was a peculiar institution, probably having more in common with the slavery which used to exist in West Africa, where many slaves learned trades or were domestic servants, than with the pattern of slavery which existed in the West Indies and America. In the West Indies and in the southern colonies of the American coast there were large cotton and sugar plantations on which most of the work was done by slaves. In Bermuda there were no such plantations, and while slaves were certainly expected to till the soil from time to time, there were no large groups of men, women and children gathered under the control of one estate.

In the case of Bermuda it is difficult to work out exactly how slaves and free people lived together and how slaves were treated. We do know that ownership of slaves was spread widely among the white people, and that the slaves themselves either did household work, mason's and carpenter's work, shipbuilding, or were sent to sea in Bermuda's merchant fleet.

The fact that Bermuda ships were partly manned by slaves was vitally important to the island's economy, for the Bermuda ship-owners, using this cheaper labour, were able to underbid competitors for cargoes. They were also helped by other reasons such as the excellence of the design of their ships and the strength and endurance of the cedar wood.

It appears that few slaves came directly to Bermuda from Africa. Some Bermuda ships carried slaves to the West Indian or American markets, but most slaves coming to Bermuda had already been taken from Africa and landed somewhere else on the Western side of the Atlantic; or occasionally they had been working for masters in Britain. In any case, not all Bermuda slaves were Africans. There were also a number of Indians, both from the American coast and from the West Indies.

The *Edwin* brought the first Indian and the first black man to Bermuda in 1616, and after that other black people were brought in, partly as agricultural experts, before the first major importations in 1619. The ship they came on was perhaps a pirate vessel; in any case the slaves were given to the Governor, Miles Kendall, as a present. Later when Nathaniel Butler arrived and Kendall went to England, Butler seized the slaves for the Bermuda Company and assigned them to his great friend, the Earl of Warwick. Thereafter there was a considerable dispute over who the rightful owner was.

White slaves were also imported as a result of Cromwell's victories over the Irish. Also indentured servants, who were bound to work a set number of years to pay off their passage money, were brought in. One large group of slaves arrived in 1644, when Captain William Jackson arrived with his fleet after a successful sweep through the Caribbean against the Spanish colonies. He brought in thirty-six people he had captured, most of them Indian women.

Most of the island's slaves were imported in the early days of Bermuda's history; by 1670 the Government was already trying to stop people bringing in any more, because large numbers of slaves were not necessary on a small island where the economy was based on shipbuilding and sailing.

By 1699 the population consisted of 3,615 white people and 2,247 black people. The figures included 803 white men and 566 black, and 1,050 white women and 649 black.

This meant that early on the Bermuda people started to develop special qualities, responding to the island, the sea, the climate and special economic conditions. The races became mixed, though not completely, so that now the Bermuda people have a wide variety of skin colour, ranging from the black of the full-blooded Negro to the white of the full-blooded Caucasian.

Despite skin colour differences the fact of living together for nearly 400 years makes us, white and black, one people.

Attempts at Rebellion

Not all Indians and Africans in Bermuda were slaves, judging by the early records. In 1656, for instance, all free black people were ordered to go to Eleutheria in the Bahamas. This was because there had been a plot 'that the negroes in this island had contrived for cutting off and destroying the English in the night', according to the old records. Four slaves and one free man, Willi fforce, were alleged to be the conspirators, but the evidence cannot have been strong because only two, named in the records as Black Tom and Cabilecto, were ordered to be executed.

However, a proclamation was issued preventing all black people from stirring at night from their owners' houses unless they had a pass, stopping black people from engaging in trade, and banishing all free negroes to Eleutheria, including Willi fforce.

This appears to be the second time white settlers had been worried about a slave uprising. The first time was about 1629. The third occurred in 1673. On Christmas Eve of that year the Governor, Sir John Heydon, and his Council found six black men guilty of playing a major role in the plot. This time no executions were ordered, but the six men were ordered to have their noses slit, to be branded with the letter 'R' on the forehead and to be whipped. Other slaves were also ordered to be branded and whipped. The punishments were carried out at 'ye bottom of ye Laine', which may be the present Foot-of-the-Lane. As well as punishing the ringleaders, once again orders were issued restricting all black people.

Apparently there were no further problems between black and white Bermudians until 1730. At that time the garrison of the regular British Army, the Independent Company of Foot, had been sent to the Bahamas where pirates were running rampant again, and there was another attempted revolt. This time a few slaves planned to poison their masters. It ended in the famous execution of Sarah Bassett, who was accused of attempting to poison her master and mistress and a fellow slave, and who was regarded as the ringleader. She has always been said to have been executed near a well which once stood close to Point Finger Road. She was brought from St George's for the execution and on the way a number of people passed her. 'Don't hurry,' she is supposed to have said, 'the fun doesn't start until I get there.' It was a very hot day, and ever since a hot day has been called a Sarah Bassett day.

The attempted revolt in 1761 seems to have caused more fear among the white people than any of the previous ones. We cannot be certain of the precise causes, apart from general discontent among the slaves but there was a series of events which built up the tension.

Early in the year a black man who raped a white woman was tried and ordered to be executed on 24th June at Gibbon's Island, Smith's, and his body was hung in chains between 9 a.m. and noon.

Later in the year a free black woman, Rachel Fubler, complained that Edward Seymour had taken two of her children. The matter was placed in the hands of the Attorney General, who was ordered to take steps to free them. The records do not clearly indicate the outcome of this.

There were also several cases of poisoning on the island which reminded people of the plot of 1730. Then the climax came when on 12th October 1761, John Vickers of Smith's Parish overheard rebellious talk among a group of slaves, in particular three named as Nat, George and Peter. George was reported to have said that there would be a great victory gained soon, or if not one-half to

A reconstruction of the seizure of an Arabian ship by the Bermudian crew of the 'Amity'—note that there are both black and white sailors in the crew.

two-thirds of the negroes in Bermuda would be hanged. It was realized that this time the plot was widespread.

The island was still in a state of turmoil a month later, and in an action which has become familiar in our own age in times of excitement, the 5th November Guy Fawkes celebrations were banned.

The outcome of the attempted revolt was the execution of six people and the revival of many harsh laws against free and slave black people.

The fact that there were attempted slave revolts indicates that a number of black people had strong grievances about their treatment in Bermuda, but the fact that none of them actually roused the country to civil war, as happened elsewhere, perhaps shows that many black people did not find their position so intolerable that they were willing to take the risks involved in a full-scale uprising.

An indication of this is the way seventy slaves on a Bermuda privateer, the *Regulator*, behaved when they had a chance to escape from the island. The *Regulator* put into Boston seventeen or eighteen years after the 1761 trouble, during the American Revolutionary War, and the crew were discharged. All but one of the slaves, who died, made their way to Bermudian ships and came home.

The Relationship Between Master and Slave

Masters and slaves often tended to be dependent on each other, and there are many tales which indicate mutual affection. A situation which must have occurred many times in a seafaring Bermuda is recorded in the case of a widow, Mrs Forbes, who was mostly dependent on the earnings of her slave, Mingo.

Some owners recompensed their slaves' faithful service by setting them free in their wills; Governor John Hope so appreciated the way in which a slave named Nancy looked after his wife when she was ill that he purchased her and set her free. Because of actions similar to this there were about one hundred freed slaves in Bermuda by the end of the eighteenth century.

The sale of slaves appears to have been rare, and the procedure was difficult. A New Englander reported that the sale of a slave in Bermuda was as reproachful as the sale of a son elsewhere.

The children of slaves became slaves, which created legal problems when slaves belonging to two different masters married. It was agreed in the seventeenth century that the first child would go to the owner of the wife, the second to the owner of the husband, and so on.

A story is told of a young man named John who belonged to a family living at Flatts who disapproved of his visits to his girl friend, who was owned by another family living on the other side of Harrington Sound.

Slaves going about at night were liable to be in trouble, so John used to swim to see his beloved. His owner discovered this, and bound John to a stake with a chain. One night John, still determined to see his girl, found he could not wriggle out of his fetters, and pulled up the stake as well and swam once more to see his sweetheart. This softened the owners' hearts, and they allowed the couple to marry.

White Christians varied in their attitudes towards slaves. In the early days of Bermuda most preachers felt that slaves should be christened and taught about Christianity, but there were slave-owners who felt that Christianity only made the slaves restless. Theologians battled about the question, but by the mid-eighteenth century, in Bermuda anyway, most slaves appear to have been expected to go to church, but were expected to sit in galleries.

Punishment for slaves was usually a flogging, administered not by the owner but by a parish official who became known as the 'Jumper' because he made people jump.

Bermuda in Mid-Eighteenth Century

The Bermuda of that time appears to have been a relatively simple, poor community. People lived off fish a good deal—salt cod with potatoes and bananas is still a traditional Sunday breakfast—imported flour to make bread, and imported or grew corn (maize).

Another local food which has continued in use to the present day was cassava (from the root of the manihot bush which is also the source of tapioca). This provided a flour from a locally-grown crop. Nowadays cassava pie remains a favourite Bermuda Christmas dish. The crust is made from highly spiced cassava dough and the pie is filled with beef, chicken and pork.

Transportation from one part of the island to another was normally by boat. There were probably few horses, and the old roads, such as the tribe roads (a few of which still exist) look as if they were just wide enough to allow a barrel to be rolled along. Flour may well have been transported in this way.

Freemasonry in Bermuda traces back to this era. Both William Popple, Governor at this time, and his brother and predecessor, Alured Popple, were Masons, and William Popple succeeded in establishing the first lodge in 1761. Apparently the lodge faded out of existence, but Masonry was re-established before the end of the century, and has endured ever since. The first lodges were white, but, looking ahead into the next century, the first integrated lodge, Hannibal No. 224, was established in 1867.

NOTE

The Bermudian   This portion of a poem by a Bermudian, Nathaniel Tucker, written when he was unhappily at school in Edinburgh in 1772, gives some idea of life in Bermuda at the time.

> *Before Aurora gilds the Eastern skies*
> *The sun-burnt tenants of the cottage rise;*
> *With many a yawn their drowsy comrades hail,*
> *Rub their dim eyes, and taste the morning gale.*
> *Some bear the basket, plenteously supply'd*
> *With hooks and lines, the able fisher's pride;*

Others with dexterous hands and toils display
Well skilled to circumvent the scaly prey;
With wide-extended nets the shores they sweep,
Or man the bark, and plough the finny deep.
The little urchin, playing on the strand,
At distance kens the bark returned to land;
Meanwhile the housewife decks the cleanly board,
With all her homely cottage can afford;
Her little brood are seated to their wish,
And taste the blessing of the smoking dish;
Of childish stories prattle all the while,
Regarding either parent with a finny smile;
The finny monster's grateful taste admire,
And for it bless their providential sire.
He with delight the youthful tribe surveys,
His gladden'd eyes still brighten as they gaze;
Of earthly joys he knows no higher pitch,
And bids the prince be great, the miser rich.

CHAPTER 11

Gunpowder, Revolution and Forts

On the evening of 14th August 1775 a group of men came ashore from some whaleboats at Tobacco Bay, St George's. They crept up the short, steep hill to where the colony's gunpowder magazine lay. Some went on to keep watch. Others climbed to the roof and broke off some slates, crept in through the hole, jumped down and forced open the door. Soon the small barrels of gunpowder were being rolled down to the bay.

The lookouts were suddenly frightened when a man in uniform approached through the night. Taking no chances, they struck him down, and buried him in the Governor's garden. His bones were found a hundred years later when the foundations were being dug for a replacement for old St Peter's Church (a replacement which was never completed and is now known as 'The Unfinished Church'). The skeleton was dressed in a French uniform, which explains why a French officer on parole in St George's disappeared that hot summer's night. The powder was taken by the whaleboats out to two American ships, the *Lady Catherine* of Virginia and the *Charleston and Savannah Pacquet* of South Carolina.

It was being taken to an America at war, a war against Great Britain which was to re-shape the destiny of the Western Atlantic and the world. The thirteen American colonies had rebelled because of the harsh British retaliation after a Boston mob had thrown tea overboard from British ships in Boston Harbour.

A reconstruction of the Gunpowder Steal, 1775.

It is thought that very roughly one third of the American colonists were willing revolutionaries, one third were active loyalists, and one third would have preferred not to be involved on either side. Perhaps the same was true for Bermuda at that time; certainly the raid on the magazine was carried out with Bermudian help. Even now however, the details are not known, which is not surprising since members of several prominent families, in particular the Tuckers, could have lost their lives if their part were discovered.

They did it because the newly-formed American Continental Congress had stopped the export of food supplies to all British colonies. Without the knowledge of the Governor a group of prominent Bermudians, led by Colonel Henry Tucker, went to plead Bermuda's cause with the Congress, since the import of food was essential to the existence of the island, and offered to bring salt to America. The Congress, not realising that salt was an important article of war, turned the Bermudians down, but said they might change their minds in return for gunpowder.

General George Washington himself wrote to the Bermudians on this very subject. In fact his letter arrived some weeks after the gunpowder had been stolen, and after it had been taken to the American continent. This was the letter he wrote:

Gentlemen

In the great conflict which agitates this continent, I cannot doubt but the asserters of freedom and the right of the constitution are possessed of your most favourable regards and wishes for success. As descendants of free men, and heirs with us of the same glorious inheritance, we flatter ourselves that, though divided by our situation, we are firmly united in sentiment. The cause of virtue and liberty is confined to no continent or climate. It comprehends, within its capacious limits, the wise and good, however dispersed and separated in space and distance.

You need not be informed that the violence and rapacity of a tyrannic ministry have forced the citizens of America, your brother colonists, into arms. We equally detest and lament the prevalence of those counsels which have led to the effusion of so much human blood, and left us no alternative but a civil war, or a base submission.

The wise disposer of all events has hitherto smiled upon our virtuous efforts. Those mercenary troops, a few of whom lately boasted of subjugating this vast continent, have been checked in their earliest ravages, and are now actually encircled in a small space, their arms disgraced, and suffering all the calamities of a siege.

The virtue, spirit and union of the provinces leave them nothing to fear, but the want of ammunition. The application of our enemies to foreign states, and their vigilance upon our coasts, are the only efforts they have made against us with success. Under these circumstances, and with these sentiments, we have turned our eyes to you, Gentlemen, for relief.

We are informed that there is a very large magazine on your island under a very feeble guard. We would not wish to involve you in an opposition in which, from your situation, we should be unable to support you; we know not, therefore, to what extent to solicit your assistance in availing ourselves of this supply; but if your favour and friendship to North America and its liberties have not been misrepresented, I persuade myself you may, consistent with your own safety, promote and further the scheme, so as to give it the fairest prospect of success.

Be assured that in this case the whole power and exertion of my influence will be made with the honourable Continental Congress, that your island may not only be supplied with provisions, but experience every other mark of affection and friendship which the grateful citizens of a free country can bestow on its brethren and benefactors.

George Washington

George Washington.

On the morning of 15th August Governor George James Bruere found out about the theft. He immediately issued a proclamation:

POWDER STEAL
Advt.
Save your country from ruin, which may
hereafter happen. The Powder stole out of the
Magazine late last night cannot be carried far
as the wind is so light.

A GREAT REWARD
will be given to any person that can make a proper
discovery before the magistrates.

Not only was the unhappy Governor's advertisement a failure; he then had great difficulty in sending word to General Gage, commanding the British troops at Boston, to tell him what had happened. No Bermuda ship wanted to sail, and when he found a messenger an attempt was made to steal the letter. However the message did eventually get through. Bruere must have felt that he was almost alone in an island filled with revolutionaries, but the situation was probably not really like that. Many of the people involved were thinking not of loyalty or revolution, but of the good of the island, and food was running short; it was essential to obtain supplies even if illegally.

Bruere had a year to endure before Royal Navy ships arrived, but when they came they strained loyalties almost to the breaking point. The Royal Navy men in an attempt to stop trade with the American colonies captured Bermuda ships, burnt one Bermuda vessel in Ely's Harbour, and sent landing forces into warehouses where they thought contraband was hidden.

In the autumn of 1778 British troops arrived, because of Bermuda's sympathy with the rebels, but still the occasional American

Colonel Henry Tucker—this portrait is on display at the President Henry Tucker House.

rebel privateer was able to slip into the West End while a British warship, the *Nautilus*, lay in Castle Harbour.

Other American privateers, loyal to Britain, used Bermuda as a base. Most of them were owned by a Virginian family named Goodrich, and at one point several of the Goodrich vessels controlled Chesapeake Bay. Bermudians did not like these vessels either, because they captured Bermuda ships as well as American.

The loyalist privateers were such a nuisance to the Continental Congress that they decided to try and capture Bermuda. Four warships were sent, and arrived off the island on 1st December 1779; a few hours too late. That morning a British convoy had put in with reinforcements for the garrison, and the chance the Americans had of capturing Bermuda disappeared. This was the only plan for capturing Bermuda which came close to success, but the Americans kept their eye on the island, and devised several schemes for capturing the colony.

Soon afterwards Bermuda was hit by a terrible epidemic. It started in prison (the building is now the St George's Post Office) among American prisoners, and quickly spread throughout Bermuda. Resistance to disease was low because of the great shortage of food.

The following year, in September, Bruere died after enduring one of the most difficult administrations that a loyal Governor ever had to undergo. He was succeeded by his son, another George, who quickly proved himself equally loyal but more energetic and able than his father. Any lingering thoughts Bermudians might have had about joining the United States were squashed, although by now it was becoming apparent that Britain was losing the war. France and Spain had joined the United States, and in October 1781 the combined American and French forces won the great victory of Yorktown. Peace was signed a few years later.

Gibraltar of the West

With the ending of the war it was clear that Britain's position in the Western Atlantic had completely changed. The great chain of ports and cities which had been available to her forces up and down the American coast were gone now that the United States was independent. Instead, they were left with Halifax to the north in Canada, Bermuda in the middle and the Bahamas in the south.

In Bermuda the younger Governor Bruere had been succeeded by William Browne, a loyalist from Massachusetts. Under his leadership Bermuda petitioned London to become 'the Gibraltar of the West'. Nothing happened immediately, but throughout the next century the fortifications of Bermuda were constantly improved, and Bermuda moved from being a sea-faring community dependent on her ships and salt trade to being a fortress island.

Work on the 'Gibraltar of the West' began just after the outbreak of war between Britain and Revolutionary France on 1st February 1793. On that day France declared war on Britain, and by June of the same year the first formal moves to fortify Bermuda had started. Captain Andrew Durnford outlined to the House of Assembly the military needs for the defence of the island. He wanted four parcels of land in St George's and one in Southampton.

The following year Captain Hurd of the Royal Navy, who had been surveying Bermuda waters for some time, discovered that quite large vessels could sail from Five Fathom Hole around St Catherine's Point and up to the West End of the island. Captain Hurd was under the orders of Vice-Admiral Sir George Murray and the big area of deep water inside the reefs north of St George's was named Murray's Anchorage in his honour; a name it retains today.

Admiral Murray's flagship, the 74-gun battleship *Resolution*, was successfully piloted into the anchorage in April 1795, by Pilot Jemmy Darrell, a Bermuda slave. The Admiral was so pleased with his work that he asked the Governor and Council to give him his freedom, which was done.

The Admiralty decided in 1795 that they wanted to build a dockyard at Ireland Island and a depot in St George's, but there was to be a delay of fifteen years before the work at the West End started.

Britain was facing enormous problems at this time. From 1795 onwards the French won a series of victories on land and threatened British seapower. One of the threats came through the commissioning of privateers, which swarmed into the Atlantic.

Bermuda vessels were captured by these ships, but Bermudians also took out letters-of-marque and preyed on French shipping and property. Particular targets were Frenchmen and their families escaping from Haiti, where a slave revolt (eventually successful in 1804) led by Toussaint L'Ouverture, Jean-Jacques Dessalines and Henri Christophe had started in 1794.

Bermuda Privateers

Among the Bermudians who skippered privateers was Hezekiah Frith, who made a series of successful voyages using mixed slave and free crews. The slaves were entered in the ship's books for a share in the profits, though probably some or all of this money went to their owners. Slaves were hired out for crews as they were for other jobs.

One of Frith's voyages ended in disaster. In 1797 his vessel, the *Hezekiah*, was taken by the Spanish frigate *Juno*. There were fifty-six slaves aboard the privateer, and all were considered lawful prize by the Spanish, although Frith attempted to offer himself as ransom for them. He was soon freed, and returned to Bermuda to build a new ship, and to go to sea many more times.

One of the captured slaves, John Graisberry, finally succeeded in returning to Bermuda in 1844, nearly fifty years afterwards. He said that all but three of the crew had died in that time, and attributed his own long life to drinking rum only seldom and never becoming intoxicated. He had endured twenty-two years of slavery in Cuba, had been released, and had finally been given a passage to Bermuda by the British Consul.

Renewed Trouble in the Atlantic

As the new century dawned the international situation was changing. In the 1790s the Americans, annoyed at British and French attacks on their ships, had armed their vessels and had sent their navy to sea in an undeclared war, principally against the French.

France however had a great prize to offer America, and in 1803 President Thomas Jefferson made a deal to buy the whole of the enormous but unsettled part of middle America then owned by France and known as the Louisiana territory.

The great Louisiana Purchase seems to have inflamed a number of Americans with a desire for even more land. Britain, the old enemy, was busy fighting France, so Canada her colony, looked almost defenceless. Also in an attempt to stop countries not involved in the war trading with France the Royal Navy was snatching American merchantmen, seizing members of their crews and sending the ships into British ports for long drawn out legal proceedings. Thus the U.S. had a good excuse for starting hostilities.

Eventually, on 18th June 1812 the U.S. Congress declared war on Britain.

NOTE

Tom Moore the Poet   When enemy ships were captured they had to be taken before a Court of Admiralty and certified as being legitimate prizes. In 1804 Tom Moore, the Irish poet, was sent to Bermuda to take up the easy job of being registrar of the court. He only stayed a few months, then turning his job, but not the financial rewards, over to a deputy, but he made a considerable impact on Bermuda.

He wrote several poems about Bermuda and girls, and addressed a number of them to someone he called 'Nea'; always believed to be Mrs Hester Tucker. A stanza of one of his 'Odes to Nea' reads:

> *Oh! trust me, 'twas a place, an hour,*
> *The worst that e'er temptation's power,*
> *Could tangle me or you in!*
> *Sweet Nea! let us roam no more*
> *Along that wild and lonely shore,*
> *Such walks will be our ruin!*

Tom Moore's restaurant in Hamilton Parish is named after the poet. He did not actually own it or live in it, but he did visit it a number of times, and one of his poems refers to a calabash tree nearby.

CHAPTER 12

The War of 1812

With the start of the War of 1812 Bermuda became a great centre of activity as the hard-pressed Royal Navy stretched the line of its ships still further and started a blockade of the American coast.

At first the Navy underestimated the fighting ability of the big American frigates, and a number of British ships were defeated in single-ship actions. Only once was the score reversed, when H.M.S. *Shannon* defeated the U.S.S. *Chesapeake* off Boston.

The Royal Navy quickly learned to sail their warships only in squadrons, preferably with a heavyweight battleship in each one, and eventually, despite the American successes, a large number of American merchantmen and warships were held in port or captured on the high seas.

A large number of prizes were brought into Bermuda and many captured vessels swung at anchor in St George's. Their numbers were reduced on the night of 4th August 1813, when a tremendous hurricane swept over Bermuda. Thirty ships ran aground in the harbour, swept from their moorings down to the end of Mullet Bay.

The war situation changed enormously in the spring of 1814 when Napoleon, Emperor of the French was defeated. Veteran units of the highly successful British Army which had been fighting French troops in Spain were detached for service in North America, and ships and troops assembled at Bermuda.

By July everything was ready, but the ships anchored inside the reef barrier at Murray's Anchorage could not get out because an east wind was blowing. A Bermudian, Joseph Nicholas Hayward, offered to pilot the ships out by a little-known channel near North Rock. The Admiral agreed and the ships set sail.

Sir Harry Smith, an army officer on the big 80-gun flagship H.M.S. *Tonnant*, tells what happened next: 'The passage is most intricate and the pilot directed the helmsman by looking into the water at each of the rocks. It was the most extraordinary thing ever seen, the rocks visible under water all around the ships.

'Our pilot, a gentleman, said there was only one part of the passage that gave him any apprehension; there was a turn in it and he feared that the *Tonnant* was so long that her bows would touch; on my honour, when her rudder was clear there was a foot to spare. The breeze was very light and for half an hour it almost died away. The only expression the Admiral was heard to make was: "Well, if the breeze fails it will be a good turn I have done the Yankees." '

The breeze did not fail, and the ships went on to help with the successful attack on Washington, which resulted in the burning of the White House and the Capitol.

Midshipman Richard Sutherland Dale

The most important prize brought into Bermuda during the war was the big American frigate U.S.S. *President*.

In January 1815 a heavy gale blew the British squadron blockading New York off shore, and Captain Stephen Decatur took advantage of the situation to slip out of harbour in the *President*.

Captain Hayes, in charge of the British squadron, guessed what had happened, worked out Decatur's likely course, and sailed to intercept him. Hayes was successful, and soon the British squadron, consisting of the frigates *Endymion*, *Pomone* and *Tenedos* and the small ship of the line *Majestic*, sighted the American ship. The *President* could probably have defeated any one of the frigates on their own, but the presence of the entire squadron forced Decatur to run. H.M.S. *Endymion* gradually caught up with the *President* and changed course time and time again to pour broadsides into the *President*'s stern.

Eventually Decatur turned and fought the *Endymion*, but it took two hours before he succeeded in disabling her sufficiently to start running again. But now the *Pomone* and *Tenedos* had come up, and Decatur decided he had no chance to escape, so he surrendered.

The *President* was brought into Bermuda as a prize, and here wounded Midshipman Richard Sutherland Dale was landed with other American prisoners. A sad tombstone in St Peter's Churchyard, St George's, tells of the kind care St Georgians gave him, and of his death; in recent times there has been a memorial service at his graveside every year on U.S. Memorial Day.

The sea battle was, in fact, in vain, for peace had been signed between Britain and the United States on Christmas Eve 1814, before Decatur sailed. But the treaty was signed in Europe, and it was many weeks before H.M.S. *Favourite* could succeed in fighting fierce Atlantic gales to bring the news to this side of the Atlantic.

Duke of Wellington's Plan

After the war there was little progress made on the Bermuda fortifications, but in 1826 the Duke of Wellington devised a scheme for the defence of Bermuda, and his plan was the basis of military plans for over one hundred years. The Duke felt that the most important military objective in Bermuda was the Dockyard slowly being built at Ireland Island. He proposed that it be fortified, and Boaz Island as well.

Next he turned his attention to the channels through which ships might get inside the reefs. He suggested that the St George's shoreline should be heavily fortified, particularly Fort Catherine, and that the entrance to Castle Harbour should be blocked by sinking a ship there. This part of the plan was never carried out.

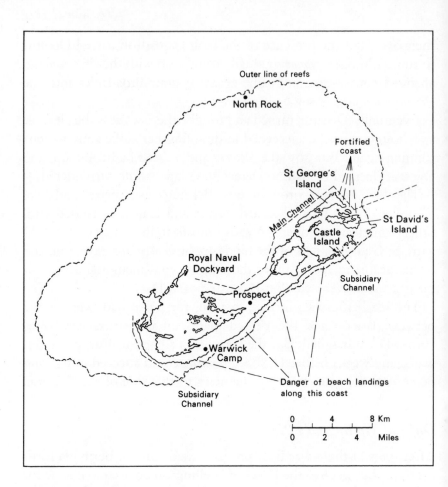

The defences of Bermuda.

Finally he worried about the possibility that ships might come in close to the South Shore reefs and send soldiers ashore in boats onto the beaches. To deal with this problem he proposed that a reserve of 400 men with a brigade of artillery should be stationed in the middle of Bermuda, able to rush to any threatened beach. From this idea came the eventual development of Prospect as a military camp.

Apart from the massive fortifications which eventually were erected in response to the Duke's plan, the British also constructed the South Shore Road to assist in the defence of the beaches.

At the tip of Ireland Island the Royal Navy erected a massive fortification known as the Keep Yard with large warehouses with immensely strong roofs to keep gunpowder, shot and shell safe from accident or enemies. In the 1820s they also built a grandiose mansion for the Commissioner of the Dockyard. They brought stone out from England and rafters made of cast iron—one of the first times this material was ever used for house-building anywhere in the world. It was so grand it could have been Government House. It had stables for twelve horses when the only way to and from Ireland Island was by boat, and a large marble bath with a great luxury for those days, running water, and not just hot and cold, but salt water too.

Nowadays the Keep Yard contains the Bermuda Maritime Museum, with many fine displays about Bermuda and the sea, including a series about the Royal Navy.

Convicts

The Commissioner came to Bermuda in the same year that convicts were first brought here. The convicts built the early forts at the Dockyard and many of the buildings.

Many of the convicts came here rather than being hung, for in the last century in Britain many crimes were punishable by death. An alternative to the death sentence was 'transportation', which meant that prisoners were sent to the colonies to work on public works. Many were sent to Australia, where most of them stayed, but of the convicts who came to Bermuda all who survived returned except one, a Mr Facy, who went into the livery stable business.

The convicts were housed in old ships called convict hulks which swung at anchor off the Dockyard with the men confined below. The conditions were little better than the conditions aboard slave

A convict bulk.

ships, and about a quarter of the men died before the end of their sentences.

The convict system came to an end in 1863. While it lasted it gave employment to Bermuda's dwindling merchant marine, and in one sad case, in 1862, a Bermuda barque called the *Cedrine* sailed for England with 200 convicts aboard. The voyage went well until the *Cedrine* entered the English Channel. There a fog came up, and during the night she ran ashore on the Isle of Wight. The weather was calm and the tide was falling, so convicts and crew all escaped safely ashore, but the beautiful *Cedrine* was a total loss. Some of her cedar timbers were saved and used in repairing the roof of a nearby church.

After the end of the convict system the forts were built, to a great extent, by the soldiers themselves.

The New Capital

It was at this period that the capital was moved from St George's to Hamilton. People living west of St George's had complained for years about the capital being situated at one end of Bermuda and on an island, and in 1790, during Governor Henry Hamilton's time, moves were made to develop a town at Crow Lane. The town was named after Governor Hamilton, and grew rapidly, for it was a far more convenient place to unload ships than St George's.

It was not until 1811 that the first moves were made to shift the capital to the new town, and the change was not actually made until 1st January 1815, to the delight of most Bermudians except St Georgians.

NOTE

British Soldiers   British soldiers and sailors had a considerable impact on Bermuda. They brought a breath of the outside world, new ideas and new ways of doing things. They gave a tremendous

The Royal Navy Dockyard today—the Commissioner's House and the Maritime Museum at the far end.

impetus to Freemasonry in Bermuda, and also to the Friendly Societies, such as the Oddfellows.

On the less happy side many of the soldiers had Bermuda 'wives' while they were stationed here, but often, because of regimental regulations, they were unable to take the women and children with them when they were moved to a new station. There were unhappy scenes when troopships pulled out, taking away the men from their Bermuda families.

When their terms of service ended some of the men were able to obtain discharges in Bermuda. It was also possible to buy oneself out of the services, but the price was steep and few could raise the money. In later times men leaving the army found their way into the Police Force and similar jobs.

The officers, too, had an impact. The Royal Bermuda Yacht Club, for instance, owes its start to the Army and Navy, and toward the end of the century, when tourism had started, they added considerably to the social life of the island.

Undoubtedly the large number of Britons stationed in Bermuda pulled the island closer to the United Kingdom and away from its former close connections with the American mainland, maintaining an Anglo-American balance in the island.

CHAPTER 13

The End of Slavery

On 1st August 1834 slavery came to an end in Bermuda. In the island it was a quiet, solemn day, a Friday, and all over Bermuda people went to church to give thanks that slavery was no more.

On that day 4,000 people on the island became free, and black people who were already free gained an equal legal status with white people. From then on, with one exception, no public laws in Bermuda referred to black or white, but wills and legal agreements continued to make a difference between the races. Only in our own time has this been brought to an end, for although slavery was over segregation continued, and even now we have by no means reached a time when the colour of a person's skin is ignored.

The battle against slavery was almost as old as the English slave trade, but it was not until the late eighteenth century that it gained its first victory. In 1772, in Britain, Lord Chief Justice Mansfield, hearing a case involving a black man named Somerset, declared slavery to be 'so odious that nothing could be suffered to support it but positive law'. There were no such laws in England, and from that moment all slaves in England were free. Not only did Somerset walk from the court a free man, but 14,000 other people gained their freedom.

Although slavery was over in England in the colonies the situation was very different. There were many laws supporting the existence of slavery in the colonies, and so it remained. After a

A 'welcoming arms' staircase.

This house, built in the traditional Bermuda style, is now the St George's Historical Society Museum.

Castle Island Fort.

State House in St George's.

*Somerset manor house, Springfield —
behind this arch were the slave quarters. The peaked building is the buttery,
used for food storage. Springfield now
belongs to the Bermuda National Trust.*

Gombey dancers.

The building of 'Deliverance'.

Crystal Caves.

while however English consciences began to be pricked over the continuation of slavery in British territories overseas.

Men such as Granville Sharp, first chairman of the Society for the Abolition of the African slave trade; William Wilberforce, who led the fight in Parliament; and Thomas Clarkson and Thomas Fowell Buxton all helped to fight the battle.

It was a long fight against entrenched interests of the time, and it was not until 25th March 1807 that the slave trade was abolished for all English colonies. Then a stronger law was passed in 1811. During the next ten years conventions were signed with other countries, and, with the final defeat of Napoleon in 1815, the Royal Navy was able to start challenging ships engaged in the trade.

Meanwhile in Britain the campaign was now against slavery itself. Wilberforce continued to lead the abolition movement aided by Buxton and backed by a large number of people with Christian consciences, particularly the Wesleyan Methodists. At the same time English economists were saying that it was bad business for Britain to follow the tradition of buying expensive West Indian slave-grown sugar when it could be bought cheaper elsewhere.

Finally, on 23rd August 1833 Parliament passed a law freeing all slaves in all British colonies on 1st August 1834, providing £20 million as compensation for slave owners, and a period of apprenticeship for slaves during which they would continue to work for their former owners.

The Bermuda and Antigua Parliaments rejected the apprenticeship scheme, and Emancipation Day brought absolute freedom. It also brought compensation of £128,240.7s.6d for Bermuda slave owners. The Bermuda Parliament made one significant change at the same time that it passed a local emancipation act. It also increased the property qualification for voting. Previously a man who owned £30 worth of property was able to vote. This was now raised to £60. Although the amount was never again increased, the property qualification remained in force until 1965 when the first act giving every adult the right to vote was passed.

The white people in Bermuda were afraid that the black people would riot on Emancipation Day, but the *Royal Gazette* reported on the Tuesday after the event: 'Four days of universal freedom have now passed; and four days of more perfect order and regularity and quiet have these famed peaceful Isles never witnessed. In one instance only have we heard of anything like a general and public ebullition of feeling, and this consisted in those recently liberated in St George's meeting on the square in that town on Saturday morning, and giving three long and loud huzzas and then dispersing, each to his respective home and occupation.'

For years afterwards there was an annual celebration to commemorate Emancipation Day.

Slavery in its Last Years

Just before emancipation, according to a visitor to Bermuda, Harriet Suzette Lloyd, there were about 10,000 people in Bermuda, roughly half of whom were black and the other half white. Of the black people 740 were free.

She writes about three black teachers in Church of England schools. One, a slave, is only referred to as Maria, but another was a free woman named Sally Socco, and a third was a man, Mr Tankard. By the time of Miss Lloyd's visit the Church of England was attempting to catch up with the lead given by the Wesleyan Methodists in working with the people and the employment of black teachers was an indication of this.

In 1800 a Wesleyan missionary George Stephenson had been imprisoned for preaching, as he said, 'to African Blacks and Captive Negroes'. Technically this was not his offence, but his imprisonment followed on his preaching to a group of black people at a tavern kept by a free black man, Mr Socco Tucker (father of Sally Socco). White Bermudians were fearful because of the revolution in Haiti eight years before and the House of Assembly passed an act against preaching by anyone 'pretending . . . to be ministers of the Gospel' who were not ordained by the Church of England or the Church of Scotland. Stephenson defied this act, and was given six months in prison. Eventually however, the act was vetoed in London.

In the next twenty-five years white attitudes changed, and in 1825 the Chief Justice, John Christie Esten, a man of liberal opinions, gave land at Cobbs Hill for a chapel to be built where slaves could worship. The work was undertaken by Edward Frazer, a slave. His owner, Francis Lightbourne, had brought him from Barbados. Frazer exhorted the black people of Warwick to work on the chapel, and men and women alike carried stone from nearby quarries to the building site. They could only work on moonlit nights and holidays, and the job took two years to complete. The church still stands. In 1829 Lightbourne gave Frazer his freedom, and later Frazer went to England where he pleaded for the needs of black people.

What was slavery like in its last years? Miss Lloyd, who helped found a Church of England school for black people, said: 'It must be confessed that in these islands slavery wears the mildest aspect of which that pitiable condition is susceptible. The character of the Bermudians is kind and humane, and their slaves enjoy many secular advantages of which the poor in our own country are frequently destitute . . . Still, however . . . the coloured inhabitants of Bermuda are bondsmen, and have long suffered the heaviest ills of bondage, a political incapacity to receive equal justice, and a spiritual privation of religious instruction and happiness.'

This view is reinforced by a story of 1828 from Belfast, Ireland, quoted in the *Royal Gazette*. Two Bermuda vessels with twelve slaves among their crews arrived at Belfast. The slaves were told that they could be free, and all except one, Thomas Albuoy, went before a magistrate. Joshua Edwards and Robert Edwards said they wanted to be free, but George Basset said: 'I am obliged to the gentlemen for their offer of freedom but I wish to return to my

friends.' The other eight questioned expressed much the same sentiments. They included Francis Ramie, Joseph Varman, James
Lambert, John Stow and Joseph Rollin.

The Belfast paper said: 'They are healthy, stout men, clean and
well-clothed. They spoke English very well and conversed famili-
arly with different gentlemen in the courtroom. They said that in
Bermuda their employment was not very laborious. They did some
work on the Sabbath days, but not much . . . They said they were
usually hired out by their masters, who get two-thirds of their
earnings, and they got the other third . . . They appeared to be
content and happy, and when they spoke of returning to their
families and friends their looks indicated the finest emotions of
affection.'

Fortifications and Agriculture

The great change took place and slavery was over. But other
changes were happening too. The period of ship-building and
trading in ships was drawing to a close. Bermudians would continue owning ships and taking jobs as sailors for years to come, but
the community was moving to a time when it could no longer rely
on the sea for a living. Although Bermuda's connection with the
Turks Islands continues to this day, the islands had been placed
under the control of the Bahamas. Also the trade in salt had declined
in importance.

The steadily increasing fortification of Bermuda brought in a
considerable income, but in 1839, with the arrival of Colonel
William Reid as Governor, Bermuda started looking to the land.

Governor Reid realised two things: that the commerce of Bermuda needed to be improved, and that it was vitally important that
the island should be able to feed itself in case of war with America.
He calculated that if war broke out the Royal Navy squadron might
be away from Bermuda, which would mean that the American

Scene on Hamilton waterfront in the 19th century—this photograph was taken in 1868 but it is more typical of earlier times, as no steam-ships are shown.

Navy could mount a successful blockade, and if sufficient food could not be grown, then Bermuda could be forced to surrender.

Therefore he worked hard to persuade Bermudians to try agriculture, and succeeded so well that by 1851, some twelve years later, there were a hundred and four ploughs in the island instead of the three Reid had found in 1839. Exports doubled in value, with Bermuda farmers exporting arrowroot, potatoes, onions, tomatoes and other vegetables.

Portuguese Settlers

It was about this time that Portuguese settlers started to come to Bermuda. The first to come were apparently part of the movement of Portuguese emigrants across the Atlantic to Massachusetts and to parts of the West Indies, but in 1847 the Legislature voted £400 as bounties to vessels which brought in Portuguese settlers.

Efforts to bring in more Portuguese continued spasmodically throughout the century, to be accelerated in the 1920s as the development of the tourist trade required more and more workers in all

Governor Sir William Reid (1839-46).

fields. The official importations came principally from the Azores, and the Portuguese were kept as much as possible to agricultural work. Nowadays the descendants of those people are an integral part of the community, working in many trades and professions.

Departure of Governor Reid

During Governor Reid's administration the British Army started acquiring land to build the great camp at Prospect, home of the mobile reserve suggested in the Duke of Wellington's plan for the defence of Bermuda.

Governor Reid left Bermuda in 1846, but his wisdom in preparing Bermuda for danger was shown a short fifteen years later, soon after the Civil War broke out in America.

Governor Reid, like Governor Butler, is known as one of Bermuda's good governors. Like Governor Butler, Bermuda was by no means the only place where he made his mark. Perhaps he is most remembered, though, for his remarkable deductions about hurricanes. Working on the basis of reports of hurricanes in different parts of the Caribbean, he discovered that the same storm would pass from one place to another. He also worked out the circular nature of the storms and told captains of ships, for the first time, what it was best to do when they encountered a hurricane. Much more is now known about hurricanes, but Reid's basic deductions were all sound.

Oddfellows

Soon after Governor Reid left Bermuda the Oddfellows, a friendly society, held their first meeting, called by Henry Thomas in 1848. The Oddfellows are an international working man's movement founded in Britain. Members band together to pay subscriptions to the society, and the society, in turn, helps members in difficulties. Frequent meetings are held at which lodge members wear special regalia for rites and ceremonies.

The Oddfellows movement came to Bermuda five years after it reached the United States, and the first lodges were part of the Grand United Order. By 1864 the movement was so popular that members took up all the carriages in St George's on the day there was a grand meeting in Hamilton, according to a contemporary account.

In 1879, with the added impetus of soldiers and sailors stationed here, a second group of lodges started under the banner of the Independent Order of Oddfellows.

NOTE

Peoples' Pleasures   In many ways the century was a time when people took pleasure in simple things. Harriet Suzette Lloyd tells of seeing Gombeys dancing at Christmas time in 1829. Their costume then was made with scarlet cloth, flowers, ribbons and red and yellow paints, and they sang as well as danced. The most famous Gombey groups, she said, were from Hamilton and Heron Bay, and as they marched down the road they were led by marching bands, the men dressed in neat white uniforms with scarlet facings. 'These musicians are all self-taught,' she said, 'and play many favourite airs with great accuracy. This is the more surprising since they do not know a single note in music. They learn and play everything by ear, and certainly have great natural taste, and love for music.'

People sang as they walked along or worked, and a number of people played the flute or violin. Words were often made up to fit the music of popular songs and even of 'Italian airs', Miss Lloyd says.

One notable versifier of the day was a woman named Pliny, and woe betide the man or woman who was made the object of her verses. The creating of popular verses continued well into the twentieth century, and today there are still a number of Bermudians who like to write poetry.

There is reason to think that the old parish verses date from the early nineteenth century. Here are some of them:

St George's:

The St George's people are so poor
They see you coming and slam the door.

Hamilton Parish:

All the way to Bailey's Bay,
Fish and 'taters every day.

Paget Parish:

All the way to Crow Lane side,
Nothing there but foolish pride.

Sandys Parish:

All the way to Mangrove Bay,
There the old maids go to stay.

CHAPTER 14

The Blockade of Bermuda

On 12th April 1861 Americans in the city of Charleston, South Carolina, opened fire on Americans in Fort Sumter in Charleston Harbour, and the American Civil War was on. It was a crisis which had been brewing for a very long time, and it was brought to a head by the election of President Abraham Lincoln, who was against slavery.

When Fort Sumter was fired on Lincoln called for volunteers to keep the Union together. The war, officially, did not start over the question of slavery; that came later when Lincoln declared most of the slaves freed, but nearly everyone assumed that slavery was the principal issue.

It was a long and bloody war, for the southern Americans proved to be able and canny soldiers who were able to defend their newly-formed country, the Confederacy, for four years against the attacks of the very much stronger Federal forces.

On 19th April 1861 Lincoln declared a blockade of southern ports; and the following year Bermuda was plunged into an exciting period which saw enormous changes in her way of life. The blockade cut off British mills from their main supplier of cotton, and cut off the Confederacy from European suppliers of arms, ammunition, clothing, medical supplies, manufactured goods and luxuries. In Europe the price of cotton soared, as did the prices of many things in the South. Anyone who could take goods in through the northern blockade and bring out cotton could make a fortune.

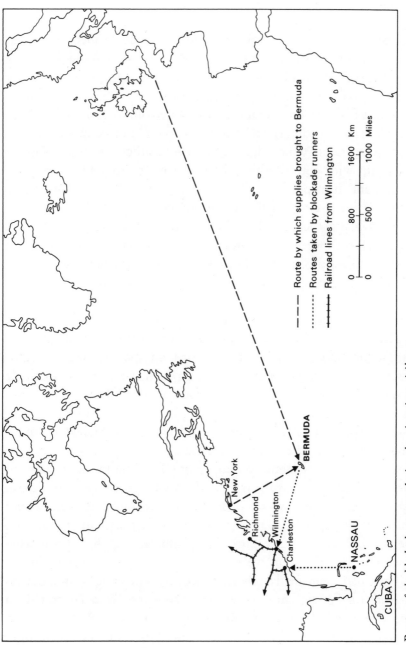

Routes of the blockade runners during the American civil war.

Route by which supplies brought to Bermuda
Routes taken by blockade runners
Railroad lines from Wilmington

Km
Miles
1600
1000
800
500
0
0

BERMUDA

New York
Richmond
Wilmington
Charleston

NASSAU

CUBA

At first it was easy to do this, but the Federal Navy rapidly increased in size and efficiency, and blockade runners could no longer be any old vessels capable of making a sea-voyage. Instead a new class of steam-ship was built which was small, low in the water and thin-masted with powerful engines.

Goods for the Confederacy were shipped out to Bermuda, Nassau and Havana in ordinary freighters, and were trans-shipped into the blockade runners which slipped into the southern ports and slipped out again with cotton which the ordinary freighters took back to Britain and Europe.

St George's, close to the ocean and commercially weak since it stopped being the capital, suddenly boomed as the goods bound back and forth were loaded and unloaded from the ships, and as the men came ashore with hundreds of dollars in their pockets for making a single successful run.

Bermuda also had visits from Federal and Confederate warships, and two very odd incidents occurred during the war.

The first warships to come were northern vessels, and they met with a cool reception in Bermuda, for many people here tended to favour the southern side. It was not surprising: captains of blockade runners were paid $5,000 in gold for a successful run in and out, and the rest of the crew were paid in proportion. Many of the captains were Royal Navy officers on leave; they helped to make officials partial to the Confederate side.

When the Confederate warship *Nashville* came in for supplies of coal the Federal Consul, Mr C. M. Allen, protested that British regulations said that warships from the two opposing sides could only buy enough coal to take them to a home port, but officials said the regulations had not yet been made official. Supplies of coal were essential now that ships were driven by steam, not by the wind.

They had been made official however, when the next warships arrived; the Federal ships *Wachusett*, *Sonoma* and *Tioga*. The squadron was commanded by acting Rear-Admiral Charles Wilkes, a man who had already caused a diplomatic incident which nearly brought

Blockade runners at anchor in St George's Harbour.

Britain into the war on the Southern side. Admiral Wilkes and Governor H. St George Ord were soon at loggerheads, each accusing the other of breaches of etiquette.

To add insult to injury, Admiral Wilkes left the U.S.S. *Sonoma* outside the harbour to watch for blockade runners. She then entered port, obtained her ration of coal, and Admiral Wilkes ordered her and the *Tioga* to blockade Bermuda while he sailed the *Wachusett* down to the Bahamas.

The *Sonoma* and *Tioga* successfully forced seven blockade runners to stay in harbour, and then managed to fire a shot across the bows of the Royal Mail steamer *Merlin*. This infuriated the Governor, but there was little he could do about it. Eventually the ships departed because their coal was running low.

Blockade running was an exciting business. A number of Bermudians served on the crews of the little ships, which would slip out of Bermuda and head for Wilmington, North Carolina. A careful lookout was kept for Federal warships, but the real excitement started as the ships neared the American coast, for there the blockading squadron drew a tight cordon around the entrance to the port.

The approach was always made at night. All lights were extinguished, and sometimes canvas was hung over the paddle wheels to muffle their splashing. At slow speed the little ship approached land, never quite sure when a blockader might loom up out of the darkness. If she were spotted the engines would be revved up to full steam, and while the stokers heaped the coal on the fires the skipper would head for shore, hoping to hide his ships against the shoreline.

Eventually, if she were lucky, the blockade runner would come under the protection of Confederate batteries and slip into the river and make her way up to Wilmington. There was always a desperate need for the cargo, which would be rapidly unloaded, to be replaced by a cargo of cotton.

Finally the ship would slip down the river again, try and sneak out to sea unseen, and steam back to St George's.

Story of the 'Roanoke'

The Confederates fought bravely, but slowly the power of the North took effect, and the southerners were pressed back. This resulted in some southerners thinking up unusual ways to fight the war.

One of them was thought up by a man named John Clibbon Braine, who claimed to have a letter-of-marque from the Confederacy. With a gang of conspirators he joined the U.S. mail ship *Roanoke* at Havana, Cuba, late in 1864. That night he and his gang overpowered the crew, shot the carpenter and wounded the third engineer, and set a course for Bermuda. He also rifled the safe of $21,000.

At Bermuda, Braine anchored off-shore, apparently fearing that the *Roanoke* would be detained if he entered port. He made arrangements for coal to be brought out to her, but found that, with a rolling sea, trying to transfer coal in small boats from a collier brig was just about impossible.

Instead, he sent the *Roanoke*'s passengers to Halifax in another brig, and decided to destroy the ship. On the evening of 8th October 1864 St Georgians were startled to see the *Roanoke* on fire in Five Fathom Hole.

Soon afterwards Braine and his crew, including a Bermudian, R. E. N. Boggs, who had been hired to help take the ship to Wilmington, came ashore. They faced a brief court hearing, but Braine produced his letter-of-marque, and all were released.

The Yellow Fever Plan

Another Confederate scheme, a horrifying one, came to light in the spring of 1865 when the Confederacy was on its last legs.

Dr Luke P. Blackburn was a kindly doctor who arrived in Bermuda from Halifax late in 1864 during a yellow fever epidemic. Yellow fever was a horrifying problem in Bermuda during much of the nineteenth century, periodically raging through the island and killing large numbers of people. We know now that it is transmitted from one person to another by a mosquito, the *aedes egyptii*, which has now been eliminated from the island. In those days, however, no one knew how the fever was passed on. Particular sufferers were people newly arrived from countries which had few or no mosquitoes, like Britain, and sometimes regiments sent here on garrison duty were decimated by the disease almost on arrival.

Dr Blackburn said he had special knowledge of the disease, and volunteered his services free of charge. People were glad to see him and he worked hard among the victims. What people did not know was that when he offered to dispose of what was thought to be infected clothing, blankets and sheets, he was in fact storing them. He hired a man named Swan to look after them, and his plan was to distribute them among the poor of New York and other big northern cities during the coming summer in the hope of causing an epidemic there.

Word about the diabolical scheme reached U.S. Consul Allen,

who told the St George's Health Officer, who in turn told the Corporation of St George's. One member of the Corporation was a southern sympathiser, and he signalled to a Confederate spy outside the window. But the other members were too quick. Suspecting what was going on, they appointed a committee to search the suspected house, and reached it just as Swan was about to put a match to the infected articles.

Swan was sent to prison for 'harbouring a nuisance' and the clothing was carefully destroyed.

Victory for the North

By this time the war was over as far as Bermuda was concerned. On 15th January 1865 Fort Fisher, which guarded the main channel into the Cape Fear River which leads to Wilmington, fell to northern troops.

There was consternation in Bermuda. Merchants who had imported goods to send through the blockade or had stocked their shops with articles for sale to the rich crews of the blockade runners, found that trade simply ceased. The blockade runners and adventurers melted away, and for years the merchants shouldered a fearful burden of debt.

The end of the war was, however, good news for one man in St George's. He was Joseph Haynes Rainey, a one-time South Carolina slave. Just before the war his father purchased his freedom, and he decided to get away from the South, and came to St George's. He set up a barber shop while his wife became a dressmaker. Business was probably brisk, but he also set to work to improve his education. Some of his customers gave him a hand. In 1865 he returned to South Carolina, and during the Reconstruction period when black people and northern sympathisers held political power in the South protected against white threats by the Federal Army, he became the first black man to be elected to the U.S. House of Representatives.

NOTE

The Curious Raft   Some years after the war a group of St David's Islanders sitting on a hillside overlooking the sea spotted a curious wreck floating offshore. Interested, they took a boat out to it and found an enormous raft, certainly worth dragging ashore for the timber and fastenings.

They obtained help and brought the hulk into Dolly's Bay. Then they tried to take it apart, but so strongly was it built that they could not make any progress. So they abandoned it.

Years later a Captain E. H. Faucon of the U.S. Navy happened to spot the raft. He remembered it immediately. It was one of three which his ship, the *Ericson*, had attempted to tow to Charleston Harbour with the idea of attaching torpedoes to it to blast a way through the defences. Off Cape Hatteras a gale hit and the raft broke away. Attempts to find it had failed, and it had drifted for six years before the St David's Islanders dragged it to shore.

CHAPTER 15

A Time of Peace

At the end of the American Civil War the United States suddenly emerged as a great military power. She had an enormous army of veterans, a large and capable navy, and her forces were armed with the latest weapons.

In fact, America breathed a great sigh of relief that the war was over and rapidly turned back to such vast civilian projects as completing the first railroad line to stretch all the way across the continent. Britain and Europe however did not realise that this change was occurring, and were fearful of the new-found military strength of the United States.

For Bermuda the fears meant a big increase in fort building and the stationing here of large contingents of the British Army and Navy; a situation which continued until the end of the century. During these thirty-odd years scientific improvements in the manufacture of guns and shells also meant that the forts had to be rebuilt or replaced frequently, and this brought large sums of money into Bermuda.

Fort Catherine as it is today is one of the earlier forts of this period, standing boldly at the end of the Narrows Channel, just at

Fort Hamilton is a good example of a 19th century
British fort—it is now open to the public.

the point before an enemy ship would turn the headland and come in sight of the Dockyard. A fort built much later is the Alexandra Battery at Buildings Bay which, on the sea side, is carefully hidden by a hill of earth. The last British fort built in Bermuda is St David's Battery, which was armed with six-inch breech-loading guns which were ready for action right up to the end of the Second World War.

Agriculture

The last half of the nineteenth century was a comparatively quiet time for Bermuda. Despite the fort building, the Western Atlantic was free of war, and was to remain so for nearly fifty years. The island for a time lay outside the mainstream of world affairs.

Apart from the military bases, agriculture dominated the economy. Bermuda onions became particularly famous in New York, with £84,548 worth being exported in 1897. This was why Bermudians came to be known as 'onions'.

Potatoes were another important crop, with arrowroot yet another. Bermuda arrowroot at one time was held to be the best arrowroot in the world, but as with other agricultural efforts here, other larger places were eventually able to outproduce and undersell Bermudian products.

Even the Bermuda onion eventually went under, succumbing to Texas growers and increasing customs duties in the United States. The only plant which is still exported is the Easter lily, but nowadays this trade is only carried on in a small way.

Bermuda was such a quiet place during the nineteenth century that a number of people emigrated, principally to the United States. Many Bermuda families today have relations in the United States.

Yet despite the quietness, important steps were being taken. In May 1883, for example, the first black man was elected to the House of Assembly. He was William Henry Thomas Joell, a carpenter, and he was elected to serve as a Member for Pembroke.

Four years previously he was one of the persons who met to found the Berkeley Educational Society, of which you will read more in chapter 22. The others were John Henry Thomas, a schoolmaster; Richard Henry Duerden, a drygoods merchant and auctioneer; Samuel David Robinson, a baker; Eugenius Charles Jackson, a lawyer; Charles William Thomas Smith, a physician; William Orlando F. Bascome, a dentist; John Henry T. Jackson, who later on became an M.C.P.; Samuel Parker and his son of the same name, printers, publishers and proprietors of the first black newspaper, the *Times and Advocate*; and Henry T. Dyer, a ferry boat man.

Roman Catholic and A.M.E. Churches

George Stephenson of the Wesleyan Methodists had broken the dominance of the Church of England and Church of Scotland in Bermuda, and in 1820 the first Roman Catholic priest, Father Boland, arrived. He came by accident when the sailing vessel he was aboard put into Bermuda in distress. Father Boland stayed for two months, and was supported by members of the 37th Regiment stationed here.

The first resident priest, however, did not come to Bermuda until 1846. In that year the Rev Dr Michael Hannan came from Halifax and stayed for six months. Two years later the visit of the Most Rev William Walsh, Bishop of Halifax, marked the official start of the Catholic Church in Bermuda.

The first Catholic church, St Edward's, was started in 1858 and on 14th April 1859, Easter Sunday, mass was celebrated in a completed section. The first presbytery was built in 1888.

Another important church, the African Methodist Episcopal, dates its beginning to 1870 when Bishop Nazery came to Bermuda. The first A.M.E. service was held at the home of Mr John Burchall

Benjamin of Park Gate, St George's. At first the church was a branch of the British Methodist Episcopal Church of Canada, but soon became a part of the A.M.E. Church of the United States.

The first cornerstone of an A.M.E. Church, St John's, in Bailey's Bay, was laid on 16th October 1879. The biggest A.M.E. Church, St Paul's, was dedicated in December 1881.

Public Buildings

The nineteenth century was the time when some of today's important public buildings were erected. The Sessions House, which contains the House of Assembly chamber and the Supreme Court, was started in 1815 and was at first a large rectangular Bermuda-style building. In 1887 Bermuda wanted to find a way to commemorate Queen Victoria's Golden Jubilee. The tourist trade had started, and visitors were comparing Bermuda to Italy, so the legislature decided to give a Florentine façade to the Sessions House; the plan was carried out following designs sketched by the then Governor, Lieutenant General Sir T. J. L. Gallwey. Included in the plan were the two towers, and the clock was ordered from Gillett and Johnson of Croydon, England.

The cornerstone of the Public Buildings, now the Secretariat, on Front Street, was laid on 8th May 1833, and the building was finished in 1836. Many people think that it is the most dignified of Bermuda's public buildings.

Hamilton's great gothic Church of England Cathedral was started in 1886 on the site of the ruins of a church which had burnt down in 1884. The plans for the Cathedral were drawn by architects Hay and Henderson of Edinburgh, and the exterior was finally completed in 1910, although further additions have been made to the building in our own time.

Another great building of the time was the Colonial Opera House, which is now the New Testament Church of God. Started in 1905

Gibbs Hill Lighthouse—a graceful example of Victorian engineering.

by the Oddfellows who still own it, it was designed by William (Sike) Smith. The building was completed in 1908.

A notable American author, William Dean Howells, writing at the time, declared: 'The two most beautiful buildings in Hamilton are the Cathedral designed by an eminent Scottish architect and the Opera House, built by Bermudian negroes, with labour and material they gave without cost, and fashioned after the plans of a coloured carpenter and mason. The Cathedral is very good modern Gothic; but the Opera House is like a bit of sixteenth-century Rome, the unpolished coral rock shining like travertine, grayish yellow and endearingly soft to the eye. The contractor and mason had read some books about Greek and Roman architecture, but he had never been off his Island, and he had felt that beauty tenderly and delicately out with his head and his heart, so that it is a pleasure to look at it.'

The building was badly hit by the hurricane of 1926, which demolished the rear section, but it was rebuilt.

Another building of the period is Gibbs Hill Lighthouse, a circular iron tower 133 feet 9 inches high (to the top of the weather-vane). It was designed by a London civil engineer, Alexander Gordon, and erected under the direction of Lieutenant Colonel Philip Barry of the Royal Engineers between 1844 and 1846.

Tourist Trade

On 29th January 1883 Princess Louise, daughter of Queen Victoria and wife of the Marquess of Lorne, Governor General of Canada, came to Bermuda to spend the winter, and from that date the tourist business, apart from wartime interruptions, has never looked back.

In the 1880s, when travel was by slow steamer, Bermuda was one of the closest warm spots which could be reached easily from Canada and the northern part of the United States. Only later, with the development of air travel after the Second World War, did warmer islands further south become preferred to Bermuda for winter holidays, and Bermuda's high season switched to the spring, summer and autumn.

Occasional visitors had come to Bermuda for their health even as early as the late eighteenth century, but the first important impetus the trade received came in 1851, when Henry J. Tucker, the Mayor of Hamilton recommended the building of the Hamilton Hotel. In fact the hotel was not completed until 1863, but its opening was followed by the opening of other, smaller places.

Then came Princess Louise's visit, which inspired the name for the second large hotel, the Princess, which opened in 1885, and which continues in business to this day.

Princess Louise stayed in the home of Mr James Trimingham, Inglewood, Paget. Her arrival caused an enormous stir, for Bermudians, whose loyalty was severely shaken during the American Revolutionary War and was in doubt as late as 1850, were now, as far as one can make out, devoted to Britain and the Crown, and Queen Victoria's daughter was the first Royal Princess to visit the island.

One tale about the Princess is that when she was out on one of her frequent walks she stopped at a small cottage to ask for a drink of water. The lady of the house said she was too busy ironing a shirt which she had to finish immediately as she was off next day to St George's to see the Princess. The Princess offered to iron the shirt while the woman fetched the water, but the housewife doubted the skill of her unknown visitor.

The visitor asked if she had seen the Princess, and the housewife said she had. Would she know her again? The housewife was not sure. 'Well,' said the visitor, 'take a good look at me now so that you will be sure to know me tomorrow at St George's, for I am the Princess.'

The housewife was overwhelmed; and while she went to get the water the Princess finished ironing the shirt.

Bermuda received a tremendous amount of publicity in the United States and Canada as a result of the Princess's visit, and numbers of people decided that if the island was good enough for a Princess, it was good enough for them, too.

Another notable visitor of the time was Mark Twain, the American humorist. It was he, after a trip to Bermuda across the turbulent Gulf Stream, who coined the phrase: 'Bermuda is Paradise, but you have to go through Hell to get to it.'

Boer War

There were a few years of excitement for Bermuda during the Boer War at the turn of the century. This was fought in South Africa, with Britain on one side, and the Boers on the other. The British Government decided to send a number of Boer prisoners away from South Africa during the war. Bermuda had a garrison who were not involved in the fighting, and it seemed a good idea to make use of the troops as guards.

However, the War Office decided to use the West India Regiment to supplement the garrison. When they arrived the British troops were given the task of guarding the Boers while the West Indians took over the job of defending the island. The presence of the West India Regiment exposed a number of Bermudians to a wider world, and strengthened the ties between Bermuda and the Caribbean.

So the Boer prisoners came, the first batch arriving here on 28th June 1901. Before the end of the war thousands were being guarded here, kept on islands in the Great Sound. A number of Bermudians felt sorry for the prisoners and helped them. Many of the Boers were excellent carvers, and there are still large numbers of cedar souvenirs around the island which were made by these men.

When the war ended in 1902 most of the prisoners went home, and Bermuda settled back into a period of quiet.

Preparations for War

By now however, war clouds were gathering in Europe and the importance of the Bermuda base began to diminish. The Pacific, South Atlantic and the North American and West Indies squadrons were abolished, and instead one squadron, the Fourth Cruiser Squadron, took their place. Bermuda lost its admiral, the station being put under a captain-in-charge.

Early in 1914 however, trouble in the Caribbean led to the Fourth Cruiser Squadron being ordered to Bermuda on a semi-permanent basis. In command of the squadron was Rear-Admiral Sir Christopher Cradock, whose arrival meant that the station was once more important enough to rate an admiral.

Sir Christopher and one of his cruisers, the *Monmouth*, were soon to meet a heroic fate, for war was imminent. Britain declared war on Germany on 4th August 1914.

NOTE

Keepers of the Western Gate　　　An idea of Bermudian patriotic feeling just before the First World War is shown in the verses of Miss Bessie Gray called 'Song of the Keepers of the Western Gate'. They are an expression of Bermuda's feeling for Britain.

> *Queen of the Seas,*
> *Thou hast given us the keys:*
> *Proudly do we hold them, we thy lovers and akin.*
> *We will guard the Water-gate,*
> *Though we be not strong nor great*
> *And our lives shall pay the forfeit ere we let the foeman in.*

> *Empty are our hands:*
> *For we have not wealth nor lands,*
> *No grain of gold to give thee: and so few a folk are we;*
> *But in very will and deed*
> *We will serve thee at thy need,*
> *And keep thy ancient fortalice above the Western Sea.*

Mighty sons thou hast begot,
Who have cast with thee their lot;
Thy quarrels are their quarrels, and thy rights their rights to guard.
We can only stand and wait,
Making strong the Water-gate
That we be not found unready when the battle is toward.

The sea is at our doors,
And we front its fretted floors,
Swept by every wind that listeth, ring'd with reefs from rim to rim.
Though we may not break its bars
Yet by light of sun or stars,
Our hearts are fain for England, and for her our eyes are dim.

Sweet Mother, ponder this,
Lest thy favour we should miss,
We, the loneliest and the least of all the peoples of the Sea:
With barèd head and proud
We bless thy name aloud
For gift of lowly service, as we guard the Gate for thee.

CHAPTER 16

Global War

When the British Empire went to war Rear-Admiral Sir Christopher
Cradock had two things to worry about; blockading German ships
in American ports so that they could not go back home, and catching German warships so as to stop them catching allied vessels.

Sir Christopher knew of two German light cruisers, the *Dresden*
and the *Karlsruhe*, in his area, and soon after the war started he
nearly caught the second one, but she was faster and escaped. Three
months later there was an accident aboard her and she blew up and
sank.

The German Admiralty ordered the *Dresden* to go down the coast
of South America and sail into the Pacific. This area was also part
of the responsibility of the Bermuda base, and Sir Christopher
followed.

Later in the year there were further worries for Bermuda when it
was learned that Vice-Admiral Maximilian Reichsgraf von Spee had
left the China station with most of his squadron and was headed for
the Americas. It was thought he might even attempt to bring his
ships through the newly-opened Panama Canal, if the Americans
would let him, and attack shipping in the Caribbean and Bermuda
area.

In fact he steamed for the coast of South America, and it was
there, on 10th October 1914, that Admiral Cradock met him with
an inferior fleet. The battle was disastrous for the British as the

armoured German cruisers *Scharnhorst* and *Gneisenau* hammered away at the British *Monmouth* and *Good Hope*, sinking both of them. Sir Christopher died with his men, for there were no survivors.

The defeat had reverberations around the world, and fear of the German cruisers permeated as far north as Bermuda. Sir Christopher, a bluff and hearty sailor, had made many friends while he was in Bermuda, and the loss of his ships, with men aboard who had friends here, led to the Imperial Order, Daughters of the Empire, setting up a memorial in his honour, a scholarship which they still administer. There is also a Cradock Road at Ireland Island.

Admiral von Spee, who had nothing but admiration for his defeated foe, himself met defeat at the hands of Admiral F. C. D. Sturdee in the Battle of the Falkland Islands on 8th December 1914. Sturdee, with the battlecruisers *Inflexible* and *Invincible*, sank von Spee's squadron, the German admiral going down with his ships.

The 'Pollockshields' Rescue

The next excitement for Bermudians came in 1915, when a former German merchantman, captured by the British and put to work for the allies, ran on the breakers off Elbow Beach, Paget. There was a hurricane nearby; the weather was thick, and heavy hurricane waves pounded across the reefs and high up on the beach. The problem was how to get the men ashore before the ship broke up.

Antoine (Tony) Marshall, a whaleboat skipper and an experienced seaman, appeared on the scene. He suggested bringing his heavy whaling gig across the land from Waterlot Inn. Fired with enthusiasm, a gang of men went across to the anchorage at Waterlot while a messenger went to Hamilton to obtain the use of Mr Spurling's big dray.

There were no motor vehicles on the island. The Legislature had banned them a few years earlier when a motorcar called 'The Scarlet Runner' had frightened a horse so that it bolted and nearly killed a man. So the dray was horsedrawn, and it took time, in the gale force winds and pelting rain, for the horse to drag the dray from Hamilton to Waterlot. Meanwhile Marshall and his friends had worked hard and pulled the gig ashore.

The *Pollockshields* ran ashore early in the morning of 6th September. It was not until 3 a.m. on 7th September that the dray with gig aboard set out from Waterlot. Cheered on by Miss Claudia Darrell, who owned the Inn and provided food and drink for the workers, the expedition slowly worked its way to Elbow Beach. Overhanging boughs had to be cut, and the horse helped over the hills, and it was not until 8 a.m. that the gig was ready to be launched.

There was still a furious sea, and Marshall and his crew, Edward Dillworth, Charles de Shield, Gordon Bascome, David Williams, Tom Basden and Reginald Minors, set out. On their first try the gig was turned over, end over end, and was thumped back on the beach bottom up.

The men were helped ashore and courageously jumped aboard again to have another try. This time they succeeded, and in four trips they brought off the entire crew, except the captain. He had gone aft to try and rescue the ship's cat and kittens, but was swept overboard and drowned. For a fifth time Tony Marshall and his crew went out—and rescued the cat and kittens.

Bermudians in France

Before the war began Bermudians had started their own military corps of volunteers, and in 1914 the soldiers went on a war footing. The two corps were the Bermuda Militia Artillery (black) and the Bermuda Volunteer Rifle Corps (white).

At first the men did garrison duty in Bermuda, the B.M.A. helping to man the big guns in the many forts, while the B.V.R.C. were an infantry unit. Over in France however, the casualty lists were growing longer and longer, Britain looked to her Empire for help, and men from both units went over. The B.V.R.C. were attached to the Lincolnshire Regiment, while the B.M.A., renamed the

Bermuda Contingent of the Royal Garrison Artillery (B.C.R.G.A.) joined the Royal Artillery and worked in dangerous ammunition dumps just behind the front lines.

There were many casualties, and many Bermudians never returned from the cold and muddy fields of Flanders to their warm island home. When there was heavy fighting in zones where Bermudians were stationed the two newspapers would race each other to set the grim telegrams in type and get the latest news to the people who were waiting in the street to learn something about their loved ones. Even worse were the casualty lists, with the news arriving by cable of the names of the dead.

At that time the cable line from Halifax to Bermuda and the Turks Island was the main link Bermuda had with the outside world, and with no radio or television stations, the newspapers were the only way people could learn the news.

Three hundred and sixty Bermudians went overseas with the British Army, and of these over forty never returned. Numbers of other Bermudians served in other branches of the British and Empire forces, and in the U.S. forces, and also suffered casualties.

Shipping Problems

One of the big problems Bermuda faced during the war was lack of shipping. The principal link between Bermuda and New York was provided by the Quebec Steamship Company's two liners *Trinidad* and *Bermudian*. The *Bermudian* was withdrawn for war service early in 1914, but was later put back on the run and the *Trinidad* was withdrawn. In June 1917, with German submarine sinkings mounting, the *Bermudian* was again pulled off the run, and a tiny ship called the *Cascapedia* was put in her place.

The *Cascapedia* was completely inadequate for the job (she sometimes took six days to make the voyage), and she was replaced by the *Charybdis*. The *Charybdis* had been a Royal Navy cruiser, but she had hit another ship and damaged her bow and had been sent to

The S.S. 'Bermudian'.

Bermuda. Here the Dockyard had given her a new bow made of teak, but she was left lying alongside, retired from the war. The Bermuda Government took her over with the consent of the Admiralty and sent her to New York, where she was converted into a combined freight and passenger carrier. The *Charybdis* took over the run for the rest of the war and for some months after the Armistice of 11th November 1918.

American Base

On 6th April 1917 the United States declared war on Germany, and soon American ships began using Bermuda as a base. A year later, on 15th April 1918 the American Navy formally set up Base 24 in the Great Sound at Morgan and Tucker's Islands, and from here they supplied convoys of small submarine chasers which were steaming across the Atlantic to the war zone.

After the war was over, but while the U.S. Navy was still using Bermuda, an American ship named the *Elinore* came in with the first aircraft Bermudians had ever seen. It was described as a 'naval scout hydro-aeroplane'—in other words a seaplane—and its pilot, Ensign G. L. Richard, took up Governor General Sir James Willcocks for a spin on 22nd May 1919. This was the first flight which ever took place here.

During that same year the optimistic Bermuda West Atlantic Aviation Company was started by Major Harold Kitchener who looked forward to transatlantic flights. He was twenty years before his time however, and although he and his associates took a number of Bermudians up for flights, the company suffered financial failure.

The attempt was, however, symbolic of the start of the new era for Bermuda which the Armistice Day brought in. Armistice Day, still remembered with a public holiday every year, is now part of our past. At the time it symbolised the dawn of a new hope for mankind, the end of the 'war to end all wars'; a hope which did not materialise.

NOTE

Bravery of Bermudian Soldiers   One of the official reports on Bermuda's soldiers was written by Field Marshall Lord Haig, the Commander-in-Chief of the British Armies in France. He said of the Bermuda Militia Artillery:

> This contingent served with the Canadian Corps during the operations of May and June subsequent to the capture of Vimy Ridge. They were employed on heavy ammunition dumps and great satisfaction was expressed with their work. Though called upon to perform labour of the most arduous and exacting nature at all times of the day and night, they were not only willing and efficient but conspicuous for their cheeriness under all conditions. Their officers rendered valuable service in the management of the dumps.

This unit also worked on ammunition dumps from the end of June to the beginning of September in another Corps. On more than one occasion the dumps at which they were employed were ignited by hostile shell fire. Their behaviour on all these occasions was excellent and commanded the admiration of those with whom they were serving. In fact the manner in which they carried on their work under all conditions was strikingly good.

Of the B.V.R.C. Lord Haig wrote:

I desire to record my high appreciation of the gallantry and devotion shown by the Bermuda Contingent, and to endorse fully all that the General Officer Commanding the Division says in regard to their distinguished record of service.

The Division's General said:

Owing to casualties this contingent has now practically ceased to exist, and I wish to put on record my appreciation of the splendid services rendered by them . . .

Five men have been awarded the Military Medal for gallantry in action, and one man, Private Noble, was promoted to Sergeant in the field by his Commanding Officer for gallantry in action on 3rd July 1916. Private Noble was unfortunately killed later on the same day.

The Bermuda Contingent has been in every action in which the battalion of the Lincolnshire Regiment to which they were attached has taken part since 23rd June 1915 . . . In addition . . . they have done almost continuous duty in the trenches. They have at all times displayed great gallantry and devotion to duty.

CHAPTER 17

Tourism

One sign of the mood at the end of 'the war to end all wars' was the decision of the United States to ban the sale of liquor. It was a decision democratically arrived at, but many Americans disagreed. This helped the Bermuda tourist trade, for Bermuda did not follow suit.

For a time however, Bermuda had a law prohibiting the export of liquor to the United States, but after a time this was repealed and rum-running, which was akin to the blockade-running of Civil War days, started. Vessels left Bermuda and sailed to New York, where they anchored just outside the territorial limits, staying for a week or more, selling liquor to anyone who ventured out in a boat and bought some. The trade had its dangers since occasionally groups of gangsters would attempt to hi-jack the ships because the profits could be considerable.

Prohibition in the United States helped to bring money into Bermuda, but more important was the tourist trade, which became Bermuda's major industry between the First and Second World Wars.

It was the British Furness Withy shipping company who played a large role in the development of tourism.

Back in 1873 the small Quebec and Gulf Ports Steam Ship Company successfully answered a Bermuda Government call for tenders to provide a 500-ton ship to run between New York and Bermuda at least once every three weeks. Between then and 1917 the company succeeded in more than filling the requirement. Starting with the *Canima*, 246 feet long, the company brought increasingly larger ships on the run, so that by 1907 their passenger accommodation had increased by 700 per cent, the tonnage of their ships on the run by 400 per cent, and the speed of their vessels 100 per cent.

During that time the channels into Bermuda were improved and, most important for Hamilton, Two-Rock passage was dredged.

By the time the *Cascapedia* was brought on the run the Quebec company had been taken over by the Canada Steamship Lines. After the war the ships of the company were in turn taken over by Furness Withy, who elected to pour money into the tourist development of Bermuda. In 1920 they built the Bermudiana Hotel as the first step in their Bermuda expansion. The hotel itself, under different ownership, burnt down in 1958, but since then a new hotel has been built on the same site.

They went on to create the Mid-Ocean Club, which still remains a fashionable area at Tucker's Town, and the Castle Harbour Hotel, which for many years was Bermuda's finest.

These improvements met opposition, particularly in the case of the Mid-Ocean Club. Although Tucker's Town was sparsely inhabited, some of the people who lived there objected to selling and being forced to move out. The Mid-Ocean was backed, however, by an act of the Legislature under which properties could be acquired whether the owners liked it or not. Many Bermudians of both races objected to this situation, but the land was taken and the club was born.

It was immediately popular with well-to-do Americans, and undoubtedly played an important role in building up the tourist trade. This was vital as the agricultural industry was declining. For instance, in 1919 Bermuda exported 91,777 barrels of potatoes, but by 1925 this had dropped to 23,448. The export of Bermuda onions suffered even more, dropping from 153,000 crates in 1914 to 21,570 in 1925. In 1930 harsh increases in U.S. Customs Duties almost stopped Bermuda's agricultural exports.

Bermuda was also faced with the problem of supporting a rapidly increasing population. There were about 17,000 people in 1900, but this rose to 20,127 in 1921 and 27,789 in 1931.

At the same time British interest in the Bermuda base was declining. In 1907 just over 1,300 troops were stationed in Bermuda; from 1920 to 1939 the strength was about 700. In 1914 just over 1,000 men were carried on the books at the Dockyard; in 1919 this was reduced to 400.

These circumstances meant that despite the hardships caused by the building of the Mid-Ocean Club, the money Furness poured into Bermuda was extremely important to the community.

Some idea of the growth of the tourist trade is shown in figures for tourist arrivals. In 1920 13,327 visitors arrived. In 1930 this had risen to 46,463, with an additional 7,668 coming aboard cruise ships. In 1937, the peak year before the start of the Second World War, this rose again to 58,646, with 24,169 more visitors coming aboard cruise ships.

Absence of Cars

Bermudians decided to continue doing without cars, in part because the tourists of the time enjoyed a place that had no motors. At the turn of the century motor cars had been playthings for the rich, but when Henry Ford started manufacturing his Model T car on an assembly-line basis and sold it at prices which were within the reach of most Americans, the picture changed, and the car rapidly became the most important means of transportation.

At first this was welcomed because cars were cleaner than horses, but as they grew in numbers they brought a large number of troubles in their wake, and many Americans were glad to escape from them. Bermuda therefore became a motorless Eden. Even the British Army and the Royal Navy continued to use horse-drawn transport on Bermuda roads right up to the early days of the Second World War. In the late 1930s Bermuda's stand on motorisation was to lead to an odd incident when the Legislature turned down a request by Governor Sir Reginald Hildyard for a car; the Governor, enraged, resigned.

Methods of Transportation

In the earliest days Bermudians had travelled about the islands principally by boat, so that when Norwood made his survey he arranged for there to be rights-of-way from shore to shore every two shares. These came to be the tribe roads, some of which still exist. The tribe roads are narrow; it seems likely that they were designed to be wide enough to roll a barrel, a system of carrying freight which appears to have existed for a considerable time.

A road was opened from one end of the island to the other, again apparently of barrel width, and this, in accordance with the ideas of the seventeenth century, appears to have gone along the tops of the hills. Roads were built this way in England as a precaution against snow drifts and floods, neither of which were any danger here, but the practice continued with the reasons behind it forgotten.

As noted earlier, in the nineteenth century the British Army built the South Shore Road from Tucker's Town to Southampton so that they could take troops and guns rapidly to any beach threatened by an enemy landing party. Much of the road runs behind the hills, to give troops protection from ship's guns and to hide their movement.

During the nineteenth century a system of horse buses linked Somerset and St George's with Hamilton. They carried both freight and passengers, and stopped anywhere along the road to pick up or put down passengers. A trip on one of these buses could be quite an adventure. Sometimes everyone had to jump out to chase a chicken which had escaped from its cage.

At the end of the century the modern safety bicycle came into existence, and Bermudians took to two wheels with great joy. The bicycles were faster than a horse, cheaper to look after, and an excellent way of travelling five or six miles.

The ferries—the first steam ferry was introduced in 1867—readily took bicycles for a small extra payment, as did the Bermuda Railway, which was built in the late 1920s and early '30s to provide faster transportation for Bermuda without motorisation.

The Government, despite opposition, particularly from owners of livery stables, decided to encourage the building of the narrow-gauge railway from Somerset to St George's. A company was formed in England and was given powers to purchase land compulsorily, and in 1931 the first trains started running. In many places the train trip gave breath-taking views, and the line had strong appeal for visitors. Bermudians made good use of it, too, but the cost of punching the line through the hills and bridging the valleys proved enormously expensive, and the company did not pay.

The railway was closed down after the Second World War, and the tracks and rolling stock were sold to Guyana (then British Guiana). There have been many schemes for the use of the right-of-way, but only one reached fruition: at the West End the right-of-way was turned into a carriage and cycle track.

Liners

Apart from hotel building, Furness Withy spent money to develop the New York–Bermuda steamship run. Their first new ship for it was the *Bermuda*, but soon after she started she had the misfortune to catch on fire alongside in Hamilton. The small Hamilton Fire Brigade fought the fire as well as they could, but the ship's seacocks had to be opened and she was sunk alongside.

Furness Withy however, had already started building the *Monarch of Bermuda*, a splendid passenger liner containing all the most modern refinements of the time. They followed her with a sister ship, the *Queen of Bermuda*, and these two vessels set new standards on the New York–Bermuda run.

The 'Betsy'

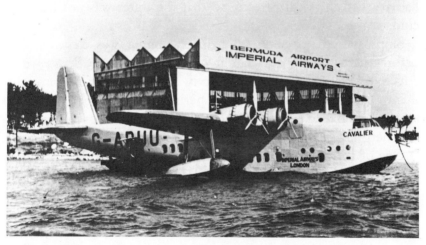

The 'Cavalier'

*The two flying-boats which inaugurated the scheduled
air service between New York and Bermuda.*

In 1938 a new rival appeared on the scene when Pan American Airways and Imperial Airways started a joint American–British airline service between Bermuda and Long Island. Pan American flew the *Betsy*, a Sikorsky S-42 flying-boat, while Imperial Airways, which later became part of the British Overseas Airways Corporation, had the *Cavalier*, one of a splendid series of Empire Class flying-boats which did great service during the Second World War.

Unfortunately the motors of the Empire flying-boats had not been properly equipped to face icy weather, and as winter came on there were occasional problems as the carburettors iced up and failed to provide fuel to one engine or another. This could usually be cleared by making the engine backfire, but on the evening of 21st January 1939 this expedient failed, and the flying-boat and her thirteen passengers and crew was forced down on the water. As soon as she hit she started to sink, but most of the passengers and crew managed to escape. Fortunately the crew had managed to radio a distress signal before the *Cavalier* crashed, and the aircraft herself had reached the Gulf Stream, so that the water was not freezing cold.

Ships started searching immediately, but it was eleven hours before the sweeping searchlight of the tanker *Esso Baytown* discovered the little huddle of ten survivors in the water and brought them aboard. One of those who perished was Robert Spence, a steward, who died eight hours after the crash having gallantly spent his energy in helping the others.

One of the survivors was Mrs Edna Watson, who later became one of Bermuda's first two women M.C.P.s (the other M.C.P. was Mrs R. D. Aitken).

Up to the time of writing (mid-1972) that has been the only crash on the New York–Bermuda run.

NOTE

The Water Supply   When ships were wrecked on Bermuda before the first settlement, the hardest task their crews faced was finding fresh water. Some might be discovered in shallow depressions in the rocks, and wells might produce fresh water or salt. The first settlers must have discovered early on that water from the frequent rains could be stored, at first in barrels and later in tanks such as we know today. They found that wells provided nearly fresh water, particularly after heavy rains. In those days the wells were built near the seashore.

But periods of drought remained an enormous problem. Tanks went dry as the water was used up, and the well-water became steadily more salt-laden.

The first person to make a considerable improvement in the water system was Sir Harry Watlington. He decided that if the fresh water floating on the salt water in Devonshire Marsh could be obtained through horizontal channels cut along the marsh, it could be purified and pumped into a big tank and then fed into Hamilton for washing and flushing.

He invested a great deal of money in the plan; and it worked. Water was piped to Hamilton and later up to Paget and Warwick, providing Bermuda's first public water system.

In much more recent times the Government has installed a distillation plant on the North Shore and several hotels have built similar plants. These provide water suitable for drinking as well as for washing and flushing. It has also been discovered, thanks at first to the faith of an American writer, Kenneth Roberts, in a man named Henry Gross who used a dowsing rod, that deep wells sunk from the hills will also produce good water.

In 1972 it looks as if Bermuda will never have to worry about a serious water shortage for a long time to come.

CHAPTER 18

War and American Bases

During the 1930s Germany, defeated in the First World War, fell under the spell of Adolf Hitler. He revived the armaments industry, developed a powerful army and air force, and began rebuilding the German Navy. Defying the rest of Europe he rapidly made Germany a threat to world peace. His troops annexed Austria and then Czechoslovakia, and then menaced Poland. The British Empire went to war on 3rd September 1939 three days after Poland was invaded. The invasion was highly successful, but after that came the months of the phoney war, in which few moves were made by either side.

For Bermuda the war almost immediately endangered the tourist trade, with both the *Queen* and the *Monarch* being required for military service, the *Queen* as an armed merchant cruiser, and the *Monarch* as a troop transport.

But even before they were taken off the New York–Bermuda run, travelling on them became uncomfortable, since the portholes had to be kept sealed in case the ships were hit by a torpedo, and no lights could be shown on deck at night. In any case, travellers seeking a relaxing holiday were not likely to travel on belligerent ships nor visit an island at war.

Although the British garrison was enlarged and Bermudians were recruited into the local forces, which went on a full-time basis, with tourism so badly affected the economy faltered seriously.

Public works were increased and the Bermuda Labour Corps formed, providing employment but at low rates of pay. The main accomplishment of the time still stands today, for the workers built Bernard Park (named after the Governor, Sir Denis Bernard) and Dutton Avenue running through it (named after the Colonial Secretary of the time).

At sea, as in the First World War, events involved ships and men Bermuda knew. In 1937 Commodore Henry Harwood, in charge of the Southern Division of the America and West Indies Squadron, visited Bermuda in H.M.S. *Exeter* for exercises and conferences with the Commander-in-Chief of the station.

The Battle of the River Plate

Two years later this same commander and his ship were to play a vital role in the Battle of the River Plate, which led to the destruction of the German pocket-battleship *Admiral Graf Spee*.

The pocket-battleships with their eleven inch guns were designed to out-fight any ships they could not escape from, and to be self-contained raiders like the privateers of the past. The discovery soon after the outbreak of war that two of these ships had already sailed from Germany led to considerable fears in Bermuda, for it was realised that either of them could approach the South Shore in the vicinity of Warwick and Southampton and shell the Dockyard without a single gun being able to reply. With difficulty a spare six-inch gun barrel at St David's Battery was taken to Warwick Camp, put into working order, and mounted there in the hope that such an attack could at least be discouraged.

The gun was never needed, but that was only one example of the difficulties the French and British faced in combating the pocket-battleship menace. Heavy ships were deployed all over the Atlantic in hunting groups, causing a serious diversion of effort.

Smallest of the groups was Commodore Harwood's Force G, stationed off the River Plate. On 13th December the *Graf Spee* appeared over the horizon, and Commodore Harwood started firing as soon as she came within range. His ships were the *Exeter*, with eight-inch guns, and the six-inch cruisers *Ajax* and *Achilles*; the *Achilles* was in fact part of the Royal New Zealand Navy.

In little over an hour the *Exeter* had been nearly destroyed, but the *Graf Spee* had been damaged and ran from the other two ships into the Uruguayan port of Montevideo.

She emerged seventy-two hours later, but before she reached the waiting British ships Captain Hans Langsdorff ordered her blown up. Two days later he shot himself, leaving behind a note which said in part: 'I am happy to pay with my life for any possible reflection on the honour of the flag.'

German Victories

Early in 1940 Germany started on the road to a series of startling victories. First Denmark and Norway fell to the German forces, then Holland, Belgium, Luxembourg and finally France herself. Italy declared war on Germany's side. Britain therefore faced a Europe united under a conqueror.

During this time Bermuda had worked hard to try and maintain the tourist trade, succeeding in persuading the American President Lines to run ships here. It was a gallant effort, but American travellers were not interested.

In May 1940 a contingent of the Bermuda Volunteer Rifle Corps sailed for England, and during the summer large naval convoys gathered here. Many of the ships needed repairs, and the unemployment problem was eased.

One tragedy of the year which is still remembered in Bermuda was the gallant fight of H.M.S. *Jervis Bay*. The *Jervis Bay* was not truly a warship at all; like the *Queen of Bermuda* she was a liner which had been pressed into service to help patrol the sea-lanes and to do odd jobs which required vessels which could carry six-inch guns. She had been a frequent visitor here as a convoy escort.

On 5th November 1940 the ship was north of Bermuda escorting a convoy bound for England when suddenly the German pocket-battleship *Scheer* loomed over the horizon. Although his ship was completely outclassed, Captain E. S. F. Fegen decided to attack the *Scheer* in the hope of delaying her so that the ships of the convoy could scatter and escape. Captain Fegen was successful, and although his ship was soon badly damaged he continued to point her at the raider as long as she could steer and move.

Finally the *Jervis Bay* sank; but the ships of the convoy managed to scatter, and many of them succeeded in getting away.

Censorship

By November 1940 many changes had occurred in Bermuda. The first one came as a result of Britain's decision to intercept mails from the United States bound for Europe.

By this time Pan American Airways was flying the only civilian air route across the North Atlantic with Boeing 314 flying-boats touching down at Bermuda and the Azores before reaching Lisbon. Mail was taken off the aircraft, and ships were herded into port to take off contraband goods bound for enemy destinations.

Censorship required large numbers of expert linguists, and soon the Princess and Bermudiana Hotels were in full swing again, the Princess as the censorship headquarters, and the Bermudiana as sleeping quarters for the censors.

The work of the censors led to the discovery of several German spies in the United States, and information was quietly passed to the American authorities.

In one notable success 270 famous impressionist paintings were taken off the American Export Lines' ship *Excalibur* in Hamilton. They were being taken from France to New York, where the British were sure they would be sold to provide much needed American dollars for Hitler. The paintings, known as the Vollard Collection, were in the strongroom of the liner, and the captain

A Boeing 314 Pan American clipper.

refused to open the door. The British security officer, Mr H. Mont-
gomery Hyde, ordered the door opened with an oxy-acetylene
flame burner, and removed the paintings. They were stored for a
time in the vaults of the Bank of Bermuda, and later sent to Canada
where they were kept for the duration of the war in the Canadian
National Gallery.

American Bases

But the big change for Bermuda came when Winston Churchill,
the strong, pugnacious and defiant Prime Minister of Britain, and
President Franklin Roosevelt of the United States agreed, on 3rd
September 1940, exactly a year after the start of the war, that the

United States should acquire on ninety-nine-year leases bases at Bermuda, Newfoundland, the Bahamas, Jamaica, Antigua, St Lucia, Trinidad and British Guiana. The Bermuda and Newfoundland bases were given to the United States; the others were in exchange for fifty old destroyers of the U.S. Navy, desperately needed for the anti-submarine battle.

Soon afterwards a U.S. survey team arrived on the cruiser St Louis to look for a site for the base. The big problem was to find a place for an airfield on hilly Bermuda, and one where a runway could be built facing south-west, in the direction of the prevailing winds.

At first the Americans thought of thrusting an airfield through the Warwick Hills from sea to sea, cutting Bermuda in half, but this scheme was superseded by another after the late Commander Guy Ridgway, a Royal Navy officer who had made his home in Bermuda, and was serving on the staff of the British Admiral, revived the idea of Mr B. V. S. Smith of using Castle Harbour, where a line of reefs ran out in a south-westerly direction. His idea was to fill in the area between the reefs and the shore, which he suggested would be an easier task and would still enable Bermudians to travel by land from one end of the island to the other.

The Americans agreed, but decided that the base would require a large slice of St David's Island as well as all of Cooper's Island and Long Bird Island and a number of other smaller islands as well.

They also decided to site a naval base in the Great Sound at Morgan's and Tucker's Islands, where they had had a base during the First World War.

There was considerable fear in the United States that Britain would collapse in the face of such great odds and Bermuda would then become a vulnerable outpost in the North Atlantic within a matter of months.

Troops poured into Bermuda, and construction was carried out at great speed. Hills fell before the bulldozers, sand poured ashore from the big dredgers, the shoreline disappeared, houses and trees

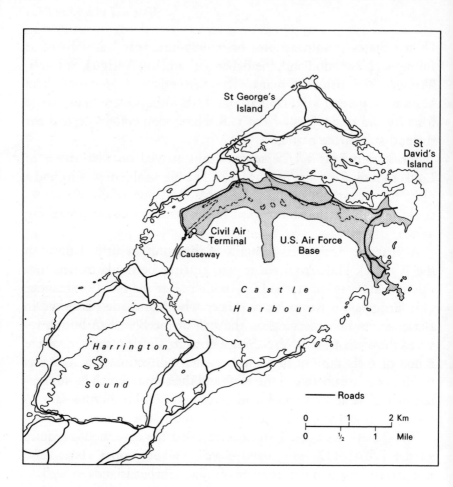

Area of the island covered by the U.S. base.

were smashed and destroyed. It was a sight Bermuda had never seen before.

Houses had to be found for the people of St David's Island, and the Bermuda Government launched a house-building programme in an area called Texas, just outside the base. There had been a plan for using Smith's Island, but that ended when the islanders made it plain that they wanted to stay on St David's.

And so the airfield was built. Bermudians went to work for the American contractors at lower rates of pay than the Americans. This was in accordance with the base agreement, the idea being to try not to upset the Bermuda economy. This situation led to the eventual founding of trade unions here (see chapter 21). Despite problems, many people prospered through this work, saved their money and helped lay the groundwork for the prospering island we know today.

With hordes of American soldiers and sailors and contractors' personnel on Bermuda the depressed wartime economy changed radically. Goods and services were at a premium, and it was generally felt that Bermuda came out of the war richer than it went into it.

Relationships with the Americans were, at first, not too happy. The dignified tourist resort of pre-war days rapidly changed character under the impact of hundreds of young men, and many Bermudians were bewildered by it. Others made high profits out of the situation. In addition, the needs of war required an end to some of the anti-motorisation laws, and soon military vehicles were speeding up and down the roads, frightening horses and changing the entire tempo of Bermuda life.

But on 7th December 1941 the Japanese made a surprise attack on Pearl Harbour, the U.S. Navy's main base in the Pacific, and America went to war with the Japanese, Germans and Italians.

This made an immediate difference in Bermuda attitudes to the Americans, and from then on there was far more co-operation as the British, American and Canadian forces stationed here worked together to win the war.

Churchill's Visit

Soon after Pearl Harbour Mr Churchill made a trip to the United States and Canada, and then took a brief holiday in Florida. On

14th January 1942 he boarded one of the big Boeing 314 flying-boats at Hampton Roads and flew in beautiful weather to Bermuda. Here he was planning to board the battleship *Duke of York* for the trip to England.

On the afternoon of his arrival Mr Churchill addressed the House of Assembly. He writes about it in his book *The Grand Alliance*:

> . . . I addressed the Bermuda Assembly, which is the oldest Parliamentary institution in the Western Hemisphere. I pleaded with them to give their assent and all their aid to the establishment of the United States naval and air bases in the island, about which they were in some distress. The life of the whole Empire was at stake. The smooth working of our alliance with the United States made victory certain, no matter how long the road might be. They did not demur.

The flight to Bermuda had gone well, and the Prime Minister was anxious to be back in London. So he decided to fly back direct from Bermuda all the way in the flying-boat.

It was a daring plan in wartime, with the uncertainties of weather and enemy aircraft, and indeed at one point the flying-boat lost its way and nearly flew over German-occupied Brest. But the plan succeeded, and Mr Churchill returned safely to Britain to continue running the Empire until the end of the war.

German Submarines

One result of the American entry into the war was nearly disastrous. Up to this time German submarines had operated mainly in the eastern and central Atlantic, attacking the stubbornly defended convoys bringing vital food and raw materials to Britain from the rest of the world.

Now however, Admiral Doenitz, the able German officer in charge of submarines, decided that the Americans were probably unprepared for war, so he shifted his attack to the American coast and Atlantic seaboard. It was a successful move, and ship after ship was sunk.

Off Bermuda one vessel packed with food supplies for humans and animals fell victim to a submarine, and during the middle of 1942 Bermuda went on very short rations. The situation was only saved when an American convoy successfully arrived; and the ships were cheered as they came into port. But it was too late to save many of the horses, and private people mourned their family pets, while carters and livery stable owners saw their sources of income disappearing. It was a tragic occurrence which made it easier to introduce motorisation after the war.

Wartime shipping had become haphazard, with calls for freighters in so many areas of the world, but as the submarine menace was conquered, and as the production of ships from American ship-yards enabled the allies to replace the ships which had been sunk, the little Norwegian freighter *Braga* was placed on the run to the United States.

A frequent visitor to Bermuda which came to a tragic end was the French submarine *Surcouf*, the largest submarine in the world at the outbreak of war. She was even equipped with an aircraft. The *Surcouf*'s crew joined the Free French (those Frenchmen who went on fighting Germany) when France was occupied by Germany, and for a period the big submarine was stationed here. Her end came on 18th February 1942, in a collision with an American merchant vessel in the Gulf of Mexico.

Another submarine, however, came into Bermuda in 1944 and stayed here. It was one of the best kept secrets of the war when *U-505*, a German U-boat, was captured off Cape Verde by an American task force commanded by Captain Daniel V. Gallery. Captain Gallery had had a chance of capturing another U-boat previously, but his men were unprepared and the submarine sank before she could be boarded. This time he was ready, and when his carrier sub-hunting force attacked *U-505* and brought her to the surface Commander Hall of the U.S.S. *Pillsbury* sent away a boarding party in a whaleboat. The U.S. sailors clambered aboard the slowly sinking German submarine, managed to disconnect the demolition charges, and, with the help of extra pumps from the U.S. ships, stopped her from going down. On 19th June 1944 the U-boat arrived here under tow. Later she was used as a 'tame' submarine in the training of allied anti-submarine squadrons.

Bermuda Troops

As they had in the First World War, many Bermudians served abroad. A contingent of the B.V.R.C. joined the Lincolnshire Regiment as they had before, but this time the B.M.A. and its wartime offspring, the Bermuda Militia Infantry, became part of the Caribbean Regiment. The B.V.R.C. saw service in France, while the Caribbean Regiment served in the Middle East. Altogether 184 Bermudians served abroad in this way. Thirty-seven died and one was reported missing.

A number of Bermudians joined the Royal Air Force and the Royal Canadian Air Force, thanks to a flying school which was started soon after the outbreak of war. They served in many different theatres of war, and had many different adventures.

The war ended on 8th May 1945 in Europe, and on 2nd September 1945 in the Pacific.

Wartime Life

Compared to many other countries Bermuda scarcely suffered during the Second World War, but there were hazards and shortages which made life more difficult, particularly after the U-boat offensive started in 1942.

Some strange solutions were found to problems such as the introduction of a sailing ship service from the West Indies. There was the summer when bread was rationed and authorities only allowed the sale of day-old bread on the theory that it would be less palatable and people would eat less. The trouble was that the flour was not very good, as it had been stored for a long time, and the day-old bread often had mould running right through it.

Shoes were rationed, as was powdered milk, butter and sugar. Rubber tyres were in short supply, and the roads went from bad to worse as the big American and British trucks and tanks rolled over them, creating large potholes. Some people used large ropes around the rims of their pedal cycle wheels, and carriage drivers cut up used truck tyres to keep their carriages rolling.

Probably the best food in the island was to be found at the American bases, and pet dogs ran off to rifle the soldiers' and sailors' garbage cans. People were encouraged to plant as much food as possible, and a canning factory was started to preserve Bermuda vegetables. Some people even attempted to make soap, which also was hard to get.

It was not an entirely gloomy time. War produces worries and sorrows, but it also produces a feeling of togetherness which is inspiring and helps to offset the sad side. It is an aspect of human nature which the student must recognise, as he must also realise the devastation and horror of war.

NOTE

War Song   A Bermuda song of the war was 'Mr Trimingham and Mr Trott', sung to the tune of an American song, 'Mr Gallagher and Mr Shean'. It was written, according to the late Mrs Knowlton, on the verandah of her house in Paget, Sanctuary, by two young American Navy officers who thought up lines and tossed them back and forth.

The mockery of the song was sufficient to amuse Bermudians as well, and more verses were added by local singers, notably the Talbot Brothers.

Here are some of the verses:

> *Oh Mr Trimingham, oh Mr Trimingham*
> *These Yankees are a blooming lot of bores.*
> *We have tried all we know to relieve them of their dough*
> *But the blighters still keep coming back for more.*
> *Oh Mr Trott, oh Mr Trott*
> *We bes' not take all that they've got.*
> *If we strip them to the peel, there'll be nothing left to steal.*
> *Absolutely Mr Trimingham. Positively Mr Trott.*
>
> *Oh Mr Trimingham, oh Mr Trimingham*
> *What's the matter with these Yankees anyway?*
> *We have given them no land, so they sucked up tons of sand*
> *And have added many acres to our shores.*
> *Oh Mr Trott, oh Mr Trott*
> *Now peace will put those Yankees on the spot.*
> *We will charge a goodly fee, to replace it in the sea.*
> *And they'll pay it Mr Trimingham? Need I say it, Mr Trott.*
>
> *Oh Mr Trimingham, oh Mr Trimingham*
> *These Americans are a blooming lot of bores.*
> *In my Inverurie House, someone burnt a chair, the louse.*
> *And the Navy says you can't sue Uncle Sam.*
> *Oh Mr Trott, oh Mr Trott.*
> *Can't you see the great big opportunity you got?*
> *For that chair of which you speak, may be sold as an antique.*
> *Where's my buyer, Mr Trimingham? At your Belmont, Mr Trott.*

Part 4

Modern Bermuda

CHAPTER 19

Post-War Bermuda

The period since the Second World War has been a time of great change for Bermuda, and has seen a transformation in the way of life, as well as a transformation of the face of the island. This chapter will deal with the outline of events while subsequent chapters will tell in more detail about aspects of the change.

It was a time when the population soared from 30,000 people in 1940 to 53,000 people in 1970. This meant that homebuilding had to proceed at an enormous pace to keep up with the increasing numbers of people, to the extent that during the last twenty-five years there has probably been more building than during the entire preceding 350 years.

The face of Bermuda changed, and instead of becoming a land of two municipalities, a few villages, and countryside between, it became a land of two municipalities with suburbs covering the rest of the island, aside from a few green areas.

At the same time the need to find employment for the increasing numbers of people led to the building of new hotels, and the requirements of travellers accustomed to the new comforts resulting from modern discoveries led to constant improvement of the old hotels.

In Bermuda the hotels were the equivalent of factories in other communities, giving employment and bringing money into the place, and from the end of the war on the tourist business was pushed hard to make up for the rapid run-down of the American bases. Even so, it was not until 1950 that Bermuda topped the 1937 tourist business peak with 61,611 visitors. The growth of the trade was rapid, and in 1971 Bermuda topped the 400,000 mark with 412,947 visitors.

New hotels and buildings were not the only way in which the appearance of Bermuda changed. In the late 1940s the Bermuda cedar tree was hit by a serious blight, and one after another the proud trees with their grey trunks and dark green foliage died, leaving their silver skeletons behind. The island was denuded, and today few live examples of these trees remain. The Department of Agriculture was mobilised to cut down the dead cedars and replant, principally with the fast-growing, handsome casuarinas. The success of this programme is shown by the tall casuarinas gracing many hillsides today, but the forest never truly recovered because of the rapid progress of building.

Motorisation

Another change came with the introduction of motor cars. After a bitter debate in the Legislature the gates were opened and in 1946 it became possible for an individual to own a car or motorcycle for his private use.

The framers of the law thought that the cost of vehicles and licence fees would prevent all but a few from being able to afford cars, but this has not proved to be the case, and today traffic on the roads built for horses and carriages seems to be nearing saturation point.

Increased motorisation also brought into question the wisdom of maintaining the Bermuda Railway, which was in need of considerable repair work by the end of the war. The decision was made to dispose of it, and it was sold to British Guiana (now Guyana).

Not only transport in Bermuda, but also transport to Bermuda changed. In 1938 the *Cavalier* and *Betsy* had given the first air service between Bermuda and New York. Soon after the *Cavalier* disaster

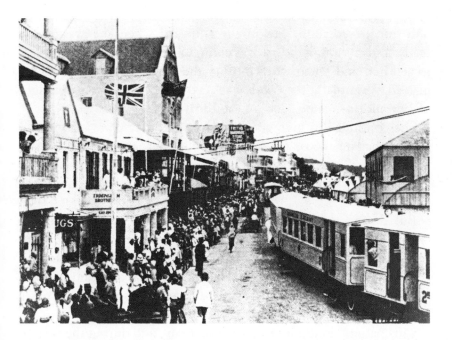

The Bermuda Railway—the trains used to travel down the middle of Front Street.

Pan American Airways brought the big, rugged Boeing 314 flying-boats on to the run, and extended the route across the Atlantic to the Azores and Lisbon. For most Bermudians these aircraft became the only means of travel to America.

The war itself brought tremendous improvements in aircraft, and military necessity led to the development of a network of air-fields and air routes around the world. Land-planes superseded the slower flying-boats, and soon after the end of the war the first airliners started landing at Kindley Air Force Base on daily schedules. The popularity of aircraft increased to the point where they superseded ships as a means of travelling to Bermuda.

Ships were not finished, however. Right after the war Furness Withy put the small liners *Fort Amherst* and *Fort Townshend* on the route while they refurbished the *Monarch of Bermuda*. The *Monarch*, unfortunately, caught fire in the shipyard when she was nearly ready, and, although the fire was extinguished, the company decided to sell her, and set to work putting the *Queen of Bermuda* to rights instead. Eventually the *Queen* was ready, and, to the great delight of Bermudians, came back on the run.

She continued to give good service year after year, but eventually, in the late 1960s, age caught up with her, and she was sent to the breakers' yard. It was a sad and sentimental moment for Bermudians when the great ship steamed away from Bermuda for the last time.

But during the *Queen*'s service the role of passenger shipping changed. It turned out that fewer and fewer people wanted to travel by ship just to get to Bermuda, since travelling by sea had become more expensive than by air, but numbers did want to make a six-day voyage to Bermuda and back again, using the ship as a hotel here.

This pattern continues to the present day, and during the spring, summer and autumn tourist season many ships lie alongside in Hamilton and St George's.

Exempted Companies

During the 1950s a new way of making money and keeping the economy afloat started becoming increasingly important. Tax laws and rules governing the conduct of companies particularly in Britain and the United States became more complicated during the years after the war, and legal minds discovered that there were advantages in setting up companies in such places as Bermuda and the Bahamas where direct taxes were slight and regulations easier. In Bermuda these companies were exempt from some requirements for companies actually serving Bermudians, and therefore they became known as exempted companies.

Carriages lined up at Hamilton in the days before motorisation.

Many of these companies are only files in a filing cabinet, but some of them have large offices and employ a number of Bermudians.

Parallel with the growth of the exempted company business an attempt was made to establish light industry at the old Dockyard. The Royal Navy stopped using Bermuda for ship repairs in 1951, although a small naval base remains. After long negotiations the Bermuda Government purchased most of the Imperial lands which had been used for military and naval purposes—for the army units were withdrawn a few years after the navy closed down the Dockyard—and planned to develop the Dockyard as a free port and factory area.

This scheme has not been particularly successful, but the buildings are there should there be a change in the future. Elsewhere in Bermuda there has been some success in establishing small home industries, although most of the products are for sale in Bermuda, not for shipment abroad.

The Imperial lands at Prospect and St George's were put to different uses, for schools, housing and, at Prospect, for the relocation of Police Headquarters, which had been at Hamilton.

As important as all the other changes which took place during this period, have been the parallel developments of universal adult suffrage and trade unions. These are dealt with in succeeding chapters.

NOTE

The U.S. Bases   After the end of the war the use of the U.S. bases in Bermuda varied enormously. When they were built the army and navy each had one, with members of the United States Army Air Force dominating Kindley, but vying with a detachment of soldiers who occupied a portion of the base called Fort Bell. At the end of the war the Air Force became a separate organisation from the army and took over Kindley. Fort Bell disappeared.

But with peace all the American services were heavily cut and the first air passenger terminal was in fact on base property.

Then came the North Korean attack on South Korea, and U.S. forces were rapidly built up again. The civilian operation was put off the base so rapidly that for a time check-in and check-out counters at the present site of the Air Terminal were in tents.

There was a further addition at the base when a Strategic Air Command squadron of refuelling planes moved in. The squadron was eventually disbanded as the Air Force moved over to longer-range jet refuellers.

In the '60s however, American interest in space exploration was sparked by the Russian success in sending a Sputnik satellite around the globe, and the National Aeronautics and Space Agency was formed. Tracking stations were set up around the globe, and Bermuda was chosen as the site of one of them. The Bermuda station continued to play an important role after many of the others were abandoned, giving important support to the Apollo moon-landing programme.

The N.A.S.A. station was placed on the Air Force Base as a 'tenant' activity. Another tenant activity to come on the base in the mid-1960s was part of a squadron of U.S. Navy anti-submarine aircraft.

Previously the Navy had operated flying-boats from their own base at Great Sound, but newer land-planes came into service, and air operations moved to the airfield.

Finally the Air Force removed their last squadron, the 55th Aerospace Rescue and Recovery squadron, which had helped not only with rescues but also with recovery of spaceships landing in the ocean.

When the 55th went there was little point in the U.S. Air Force continuing to run the base, so the U.S. Navy took it over, and at the same time retained their West End base.

CHAPTER 20

Political and Constitutional Change

The 1950s and 1960s were a time of great political change in Bermuda, a period when the traditional ways by which the Bermuda community was governed came to an end.

When King Charles II dissolved the Bermuda Company and Bermuda became a royal colony, the form of government followed that of most colonies at the time. The Governor had executive power and the right to veto laws passed by the Legislature, but he could not force the Legislature to pass laws. Nor could he force them to vote for taxes or agree to spending money for objects with which they disagreed.

The Governor ran the executive side of government with the aid of a council he picked himself; the council also had to approve laws coming from the lower house, the House of Assembly.

The constitution remained this way right up to 1968 with a few small changes. The principal one came in 1888 when the council was divided into an Executive Council presided over by the Governor, and a Legislative Council presided over by the Chief Justice. The Legislative Council was solely concerned with passing laws, but by tradition was not supposed to interfere with money bills.

The preservation of this ancient constitution for so long a time was quite remarkable. It outlasted the American Revolution, and the period during the nineteenth century when Britain brought many such constitutions to an end. In view of the importance of the Bermuda base this was a particularly striking situation. In the early twentieth century Bermuda, the Bahamas and Barbados were unique in the Empire for retaining this form of government.

Barbados first moved toward executive power for the House of Assembly in 1946, and the Bahamas followed in 1964. Bermuda came last. Now Barbados, largest of the three, has gained independence, and the Bahamas obtained it in 1973. Whether Bermuda, the smallest and most northerly, will either seek independence or obtain it remains a question for the future.

Black Representation

Bermuda's franchise also remained unchanged for the greater part of the period. By 1834 those who owned land worth £30 or more could vote, but in that year of emancipation the Legislature increased the requirement to £60, in what was obviously a move to keep white people in power.

Responding to this situation, black people banded together in political associations, and often voted for one man out of four running in any parish. This practice, known as plumping, was a powerful weapon, and helped to increase the number of black people in the Legislature in this century.

The first black man to become a Member of the Colonial Parliament was Mr William Henry Thomas Joell, a carpenter, who was elected in 1883. Another early black M.C.P. was Mr John Henry T. Jackson, a grocer. They broke down the door, but felt they relied on white voters as well as black ones to become Members of the Assembly.

Gradually black representation in the House increased, but it was only in the 1950s that black M.C.P.s were able to make their voices and views strongly felt. That this occurred was due in part to changes in the world outside Bermuda, in part to the influence of the Second World War and the U.S. bases, but perhaps more than any of these, to the influence of Dr Edgar Fitzgerald Gordon.

Dr Gordon was elected to the House of Assembly in 1943, having failed to gain a seat many years earlier. In 1944 he accepted the leadership of the Bermuda Workers Association (see next chapter) and had an immediate influence, vastly increasing its membership. The following year Dr Gordon organised a series of meetings in every parish at which he proposed that a petition should be sent to London asking for a Royal Commission to investigate conditions here. The petition became the basis for a British Government document called Command Paper 7093.

It was a tremendous effort; but at the time it fell flat. The Legislature considered the petition and issued a report on it: and that was about all. Changes were still many years away.

There had, however, already been one change: after a long campaign in the twenties and thirties, Bermuda women landowners were granted the right to vote in 1944.

Dr Gordon failed in two bids to be re-elected in 1948, but there were scenes at the polls in Southampton and St George's (different parishes had different voting days) which foreshadowed events to come.

In 1953 Dr Gordon tried again, and succeeded in being elected, along with nine other black people, the largest black representation in the House up to that date. Among the M.C.P.s were Mr W. L. Tucker, who was to become the leader in the Legislature of the movement for universal adult suffrage (one vote for every adult), Mr E. T. Richards (later Sir Edward Richards) who in 1972 became Government Leader, and Mr Walter Robinson, in 1972 Parliamentary Leader of the Progressive Labour Party.

Dr Gordon died in 1955, but he had left an indelible mark on the community. His leadership had at times been rejected, but his drive and showmanship and courage made a strong impact on Bermuda. He not only gave a tremendous impetus to the long

Mrs Lois Browne-Evans, LL.B., J.P., M.P., Leader of the Opposition.

battle for racial desegregation, but he also did the same with the trade union movement. He is thus one of the major figures of Bermuda history.

The Turning Point of 1959

In the 1958 election his loss was felt, when the number of black representatives dropped from nine to six, but the following year was an important one in this era of change.

It was the 350th anniversary of Sir George Somers' wreck, and to commemorate it two plays were put on: *This Island's Mine*, based on Shakespeare's *Tempest*, and *My Heart Stays Here*, based on the *Sea Venture* story. Both names became rallying cries, particularly *This Island's Mine*.

During the year a group of young black people, led by Dr E. Stanley D. Ratteray (later to become a Member of the Executive Council) decided that it was time the movie theatres were desegregated, and organised a boycott. It started on the evening of 15th June, and was so successful that on 2nd July the theatres were desegregated.

There had already been plans to desegregate the theatres when the large new Rosebank Theatre was opened in about three months time, but the group who organised the boycott, who remained anonymous during it and afterwards, argued that if desegregation could take place in three months time there was no reason why it should not take place immediately.

The boycott paid an unexpected dividend. The major hotels and most of the restaurants also desegregated their public rooms.

Among the leaders of the group, in addition to Dr Ratteray, were Mr Clifford Wade, Mr and Mrs Rudolph Commissiong, Mr and Mrs Lancelot Swan, Mr William Francis, Mr Coleridge Williams, Mr Eldridge Woods, Mr Gerald Harvey and Mr and Mrs Edward Williams.

In fact, 1959 was an important turning point. After that date white-owned firms which had only employed white people in offices and behind counters started employing black people too, following the slow lead the Civil Service had given a few years earlier.

In the same year, and before the theatre boycott took place, Mr W. L. Tucker was made a member of the Executive Council, the first black man to achieve this position. He was already chairman of a committee which was considering if, and how, the franchise should be extended.

Sir Henry Tucker, K.B.E., J.P., M.C.P., former Government Leader.

The Hon. Sir Edward Richards, C.B.E., M.C.P., former Premier.

The Hon. Sir John Sharpe, C.B.E., J.P., M.P., former Premier.

The Hon. J. David Gibbons, J.P., M.P., former Premier.

In May 1960 his committee made an interim report urging that the franchise should be based on the size of a lot of land, not its value, that leaseholders should have the right to vote, and that plural voting (voting in more than one parish if land were owned in more than one parish) should be ended.

Movement for Universal Adult Suffrage

It was a compromise, but Bermuda was changing faster than that. There was a considerable amount of disappointment that the committee had not called for a greater widening of the franchise, and a group of people formed the Committee for Universal Adult Suffrage.

Leader of the group and moving force behind it was Mr Roosevelt Brown, and other leading members were Mr Mansfield Brock, Mr Edward DeJean, Dr Ratteray, Mr Walter Robinson, Mr Coleridge Williams and Mr Leon Williams. The public battle was led by Mr Brown. For two months he acted as chairman of a series of meetings at which the views both of people who wanted 'one-man, one-vote' and those who wished to retain the land franchise were given.

Working behind the scenes, and then in front of them when he was appointed a member of the Legislative Council and later the Executive Council, the late Dr Eustace Cann played a vital part, inspiring and advising the leaders of the movement.

Slowly the movement caught on until large numbers of people were going to meetings. While the meetings were continuing a fresh idea was proposed namely the plus vote. Under this scheme everyone would have a vote, but landowners, college graduates, people who had served in the armed forces, and those who had attained certain other qualifications, would be given an additional vote for each qualification.

Mr Ottiwell A. Simmons, M.P., President of the Bermuda Industrial Union.

When the meetings ended there was a period of calm on the political front as the community digested the importance of the C.U.A.S. meetings. Mr W. L. Tucker himself was suffering from a serious illness which in a few years was to take his life.

Progress continued however. In May 1961 a bill was passed preventing restaurants from discriminating between individuals on the basis of race, creed or colour. This important bill was the work of a legislative committee chaired by Mr E. T. Richards.

On 14th June the franchise committee reported again. This time the majority of the committee recommended universal suffrage at the age of twenty-one, but a minority called for the voting age to be raised to twenty-five, and that electoral districts be set up with the idea of ensuring that the white minority of Bermudians should be 'protected'.

It was not until 1963 that the new franchise bill became law. Under it every adult over twenty-five had a vote, the island was divided into eighteen electoral districts (two for each parish) and landowners gained an additional 'plus' vote.

Development of Political Parties

The election that year saw the birth of the first proper political party, the Progressive Labour Party. Opposing it during the election was a loose group known as the 'Voters' Association'. The P.L.P. gained six seats, putting five black and one white member into the House. Six other black people also won seats.

Soon after the new Assembly started work the United Bermuda Party was formed and gained the support of twenty-four M.C.P.s, thus controlling the House.

The U.B.P., like the P.L.P. before it, was formed as a party embracing members of both races. They chose Sir Henry Tucker as their leader. Long active in Bermuda politics, Sir Henry, a banker, had played a vital part in the behind-the-scenes negotiations which led to universal adult suffrage. A leading member of

The Hon. John W. D. Swan, J.P., M.P.

the white group who wielded the greatest amount of power, he appreciated the need for Bermuda to change, and was not, like many other white people, afraid that political change would mean trouble and economic setbacks for the island.

Dr Gordon was the man who gave the big push to change; Sir Henry was the man who accepted it, and moulded life in Bermuda into a new image.

The U.B.P. quickly decided that the time had come for a change of Bermuda's unwritten constitution. They also decided to abolish the plus vote and reduce the voting age to twenty-one. These changes were made and a joint select committee of the House and Legislative Council was set up to consider a new constitution.

In November 1966 three members of the Legislative Council and fifteen members of the House of Assembly met in London with Mr Fred Lee, Secretary of State for the Colonies, Mr John Stonehouse, Parliamentary Under-Secretary of State, for a constitutional conference. Also present was the Governor, Lord Martonmere.

The fifteen members of the House were eight members of the U.B.P., three members of the P.L.P., and four independents.

The New Constitution

In the end a majority of the Bermudians agreed on a new constitution which brought a cabinet system of government to Bermuda. The principal points of the constitution were that responsibility for all executive aspects of government except foreign affairs, defence and internal security (including the Police Force) fell on the Executive Council which in turn was responsible to the House of Assembly, which could force the members of the Executive Council to resign.

The Council was appointed by the Governor who had to follow the suggestions made to him by the Government Leader, the leader of the majority group in the House of Assembly. The Legislative Council was also nominated by the Governor, and consisted of eleven members, four appointed at the suggestion of the Government Leader, two appointed at the suggestion of the Opposition Leader, and five by the Governor at his own discretion.

It was also agreed at this time that there should be a revision of electoral boundaries, and that four more seats should be given to Pembroke, the parish with the most people, raising the number of members of the House to forty.

The change was made in time for the 1968 election, which saw thirty members of the U.B.P. returned to office, ten members of the P.L.P. and no independents. A new political party emerged before the election, the Bermuda Democratic Party, but they failed to win any seats.

Immediately after the election the new constitution came into effect; the only change since then has been a further revision of constituency boundaries.

At the end of 1971 Sir Henry Tucker resigned as Government Leader and was succeeded by Sir Edward Richards, a move which was widely hailed as showing that the U.B.P. was genuinely bi-racial.

Under Sir Edward's leadership the U.B.P. gained a second election victory in 1972. The election was remarkable in that both parties held on to the constituencies they had gained in 1968. There were some fresh faces when the Assembly re-assembled after the election, but the strength of the parties remained absolutely the same.

In 1976, however, under the leadership of Mr Jack Sharpe, the U.B.P. lost four seats to the P.L.P., and soon afterward lost another in a by-election. By now the U.B.P. was suffering from internal disagreements, and as a result Mr David Gibbons replaced the Premier, now Sir John Sharpe, and appeared to be successful in welding the party together.

Early in 1982 Mr Gibbons stepped down, and the party elected Mr John Swan in his place. The transition was a smooth one, and during the first months of his administration the new Premier appeared to be establishing a strong popularity.

Meanwhile the P.L.P. was changing. It tried harder to appeal to middle-of-the-road voters and in 1980 succeeded in making many gains, so that the make-up of the House of Assembly became eighteen P.L.P. members and twenty-two U.B.P. members.

The Constitution, too, had been revised. The Executive Council became the Cabinet, the political heads of Government Departments were named Ministers, and the Legislative Council became the Senate, with the number of independent members sitting in it reduced to three, and the opposition members increased to three.

NOTE

Miss Eva Hodgson, in *Second-class citizens; First-class men*, a book which covers much of this period, quotes a poem written by Dr Gordon early in his career. It was entitled 'If I should die', and reveals the sadness of a man who, at that point, felt that he had been deserted by many who should have been his friends.

> *If I should die*
> *How kind you all would grow.*
> *I would not have one foe.*
> *There are no words too beautiful to say*
> *Of one who goes evermore away*
> *Across that ebbing tide which has*
> *No flow.*
>
> *With that new lustre*
> *My good deeds would glow.*
> *If faults were mine, no one would call them so . . .*
>
> *Ah friends! Before my listening ear lies low,*
> *While I can hear and understand, bestow*
> *That gentle treatment and fond love,*
> *I pray*
> *The lustre of who late though radiant way*
> *Would gild my grave with mocking light, I know,*
> *If I should die.*

CHAPTER 21

The Growth of Trade Unions

Trade unions came late to Bermuda, although attempts to put pressure on employers had occurred many times in the past. For instance, in 1863, a group of black people employed in St George's by the southern Confederate Government went on strike for higher wages. The Confederate agent, Major Norman Walker, hired white people to do the work instead. The black workers however continued their strike. 3,000 bales of cotton were destroyed by fire. Guards were stationed by Major Walker. Finally the workers gave in and returned to work.

Of the unions existing in Bermuda today, the first was the Bermuda Union of Teachers—now the Amalgamated Bermuda Union of Teachers—which was organised on 1st February 1919. It worked hard to improve conditions for teachers and for better schools. During the 1950s a second union, the Teachers Association of Bermuda, was formed, but eventually the two unions amalgamated.

Industrial trade unionism appeared on the scene much later. Curiously enough, Bermuda trade unionism started partly as a result of employment problems which developed from another group of Americans; these were the base contractors of the Second World War, and the U.S. Army and Navy.

When the Americans planned to build their bases the Bermuda Government was told that it was common American practice to pay local rates of pay to workers on bases, as certified by local

Governments. Soon after, it was discovered that rates at the base were in excess of Bermuda rates, and the pay for unskilled labourers was accordingly dropped to five shillings a day.

This however, was the cut rate at which labourers had been employed by the Bermuda Government when the war and the drastic cut in the tourist business had created considerable unemployment, and by now prices were going up as war-time shortages had developed.

A big meeting was held at the Oddfellows Hall in Hamilton on 4th December 1940, with Mr Russell L. Pearman, who was later to be an M.C.P., in the chair. The meeting agreed to form themselves into the Bermuda Workers Association, a name suggested by Mr Walton St George Brown. Others who played an important role in the formation of the B.W.A. were Mr Gerald Brangman, Mr Henry Stovell and Mr Wycliffe Stovell.

The B.W.A. succeeded in improving wage rates at the U.S. bases, and then interest in it dwindled, until in 1944 it had fallen to 200 members. It was in that year that Dr Gordon was asked to become president, and under his vigorous leadership the membership increased to 5,000 in 1945.

In 1946 Dr Gordon started his campaign to petition for constitutional and social change, and in the same year the Legislature passed Bermuda's first Trade Union and Disputes Act. The first union to register was the B.U.T.

Under the act trade unions could not be political organisations, and as a result the Bermuda Industrial Union was formed out of the membership of the B.W.A. The B.W.A. continued in being as the political arm for some years, but has now gone out of existence.

The B.I.U. was born; but it was not healthy. It failed to attract many members of the B.W.A., partly because wages by now had caught up with price increases.

Most of the members of the new union were dock workers, and in 1948 they went on strike for higher wages. The stevedoring firms managed to obtain the services of other people, including shop

Dr E. F. Gordon.

assistants who were released from their normal work by store owners, but in the end there were negotiations between the B.I.U. and management which settled the dispute.

The successful outcome of the strike led to an increase in B.I.U. members to just over 1,000, but in the year of Dr Gordon's death, 1955, membership suddenly dropped to twenty-six.

The events of 1959 however, changed the situation, and membership grew once more. In the same year there was a second dock strike, which reached deadlock while ships continued to be unloaded by non-union labour.

The strikers decided to try strong tactics, armed themselves with sticks and demonstrated outside Police Headquarters (then in Hamilton), later marching on No. 1 Shed. The Riot Act was read twice, and at No. 1 Shed the strikers encountered the Police Riot Squad, the first time such a group had been called out in Bermuda. The confrontation fortunately passed off peacefully, and finally the strikers dispersed.

Soon afterwards a number of dockworkers formed the Bermuda Dock Workers Union, splitting off from the B.I.U.

By 1960 there were approximately 900 members in all unions in Bermuda, but this included, because of the way the law was written, the Bermuda Employers Council, a management group.

Turning Point

During the early 1960s the B.I.U. began to mature, sending officials abroad for training and recruiting members.

Then, in 1965, came an important turning point in the history of trade unionism in Bermuda when the B.I.U. called on the Bermuda Electric Light Company to recognise them as bargaining agent.

The Electric Light Company said it would grant recognition if sixty per cent of its hourly-paid workers voted for the union, while the union called for over fifty per cent, and only workers in certain sectors of the company's operation.

The B.I.U. called its members out on strike, and after ten days called on three other divisions to come out in sympathy. This led to a picket line of some 300 people, and on the fateful 2nd February 1965 the tensions which had developed, erupted into violence.

The police arrested the B.I.U. president and two pickets, and soon afterwards a riot occurred in which one policeman was very seriously hurt. The riot squad was called out, and the pickets dispersed to the Devonshire Recreation Club, where they were joined by many others who also downed tools.

What had been a union dispute quickly created racial tensions, and the Reserve Constabulary, the Bermuda Rifles (formerly the Bermuda Volunteer Rifle Corps) and the Bermuda Militia Artillery were mobilised to keep the peace.

During this time non-B.I.U. workers at the Electric Light Company who were in fact the majority, for the B.I.U. had only eighty members plus a number of sympathisers on the staff of 231, kept electricity flowing to the community. This was a tense time for them, and they formed a rival union, the Electrical Supply Trade Union.

The strike ended when the Electric Light Company management agreed to negotiate with whichever union commanded a majority of the workers, and in the subsequent ballot the E.S.T.U. won.

It was the worst strike and the worst violence that Bermuda had ever known. The B.I.U. lost the battle, but it won the war. Since then union recognition has normally been based on a simple majority whenever a secret ballot has been taken, and from that time the B.I.U. has generally managed to increase its numbers until, in 1969, 3,494 members were recorded.

At the same time relations between union and management have considerably improved. Unions became part of the normal fabric of life, no longer being regarded by managements with suspicion as subversive elements in Bermuda life, and unions learned much more about negotiating techniques.

Never again have such large picket lines assembled as the 300 who were outside the Electric Light Company on 2nd February, but at the same time most managements have stopped operations when faced by a strike, which is now seen as the workers' method of bringing pressure rather than the next thing to a riot.

By 1969 the B.I.U. reported collective agreements with sixty-three employers. Total membership in all unions (excluding the Bermuda Employers Council and the Hotel Employers of Bermuda) was reaching up towards the 5,000 mark. In 1979 the number of members of all unions had increased to 7,071.

Notable figures in the trade union story, apart from the towering figure of Dr Gordon, include Mr Ira Phillip, who succeeded Dr Gordon as Secretary-General, Mr Martin T. Wilson, who was president during some of the most difficult times; Mr Joe Mills who led the longshoremen in the early days; Mr Robert T. Johnston, president for many years; Dr Barbara Ball, a white woman who joined B.I.U. in the early 1960s and became Secretary-General, a post she held for many years, relinquishing it to become Research Officer for the B.I.U.; Mr Ottiwell Simmons, current president, in 1981 President of the B.I.U. and the leading figure in Bermuda trade unionism; Mr Eugene Blakeney, who moved from the B.I.U. to become the principal official for the Bermuda Public Service Association, and Mr Reid Simmons.

Although the 1965 riot was a hard and bitter time for the community, which nearly broke into two hostile racial groups, in fact the development of trade unionism in Bermuda shows a much greater readiness on the part of both management and labour to get along than has occurred in most other countries, where labour has had to fight many harsh battles to gain acceptance.

The movement came late to Bermuda which probably helped, making Bermudians conversant with unionism before unions actually started. The B.U.T., in particular had a long and peaceful history.

In a brief period of twenty-five years trade unions developed out of a Workers Association whose president declared that it was not a union into a full-fledged part of the community.

A significant victory for the B.I.U. and other unions in recent years was the introduction of an 'agency shop'. Under agency shop agreements all employees of a business have union dues deducted from their pay, but those who prefer can decide to have their money go to a charity instead of the union. This helped to improve trade union finances, so that more permanent staff could be hired to handle bargaining sessions and disputes. At the same time, however, the law prevented 'closed shop' agreements, under which every employee has to be a member of a trade union.

Although industrial relations in Bermuda have been generally good, protracted negotiations between the Government and the B.I.U. over the wages of hospital workers and Government industrial workers brought about a general strike in late April and early May 1981 which, for the first time, included all hotel workers. Partly as a result of this, Bermuda had a reduced number of visitors for the year compared to 1980.

CHAPTER 22

The Story of Education

The period of change from the end of the Second World War to the present was as marked in education as it was in many other areas of life in Bermuda, but the story goes back much further than that.

Many members of the Bermuda Company and many early settlers had absorbed the views of the Puritans in England. One of the things the Puritans believed in was education, and among their early actions in New England, for example, was the establishment of Harvard College.

In Bermuda the company decided to set aside land for school purposes, and one of the shareholders, Sir Nathaniel Rich, gave nearly half his shares of land to be occupied by a school and to help maintain it. Sir Nathaniel thought a school in Bermuda would be useful for training Indians from the mainland as well; a scheme which, with variations, was to crop up several more times.

In 1663 three schoolhouses were in fact built. Each was fourteen feet by sixteen feet and provided with a chimney. One of these still exists, and forms part of Warwick Academy.

Richard Norwood the surveyor was the most noted Bermuda schoolteacher of this era. He had taught in England, and was the author of several books.

After the company era education seems to have slumped. Bermuda's leaders were not educated men, and teaching became a second job for the clergy, and sometimes other people would help.

There was one far-reaching plan which might have helped Bermuda enormously. This was the scheme conceived by Bishop George Berkeley, who on 1st June 1725 obtained a charter from King George I to build a college to be known as St Paul's in Bermuda. St Paul's would have educated Americans and Indians as well as Bermudians up to Master of Arts standard. Unfortunately the money was not forthcoming, and although the Bishop crossed the Atlantic and lived for a period in Rhode Island, he never reached Bermuda.

But a period of change was on the way, and as the eighteenth century reached its end the Rev John Stephenson arrived in Bermuda.

Missionary Education

Stephenson was a Methodist, and the Methodists, like their Puritan predecessors of the previous century, were interested in education. Although Stephenson was hounded out of the island, as related earlier, he was succeeded by the Rev Joshua Marsden who began to educate poor people and slaves. Other Methodist ministers followed, and by 1832 the Methodists had nine Sunday Schools functioning staffed by fifty white and sixteen black teachers with 283 slave children, 184 free black children and 96 white children attending. These Sunday Schools taught reading and writing as well as the scriptures.

The Church of England followed the Methodists into the education field, and at the time of Harriet Suzette Lloyd's visit (1829 to 1831) Archdeacon (later Bishop) Spencer had set up a number of schools and 1,000 black people were receiving instruction in them. Archdeacon Spencer, who did much to mould the Bermuda community of the mid-nineteenth century, was assisted from England by the Society for the Religious Instruction of Negroes.

Government Interest in Education

In 1837 the Chief Justice, John Christie Esten, proposed a far-reaching plan for the education of all children in Bermuda, arguing that the training of the children of former slaves was a moral obligation on white people. He wrote:

> . . . through seven generations have they not been our obedient and attached slaves? For us and our ancestors they have risen early and late taken rest; they toiled through the live-long summer's day and in the sweat of their faces they have eaten the bread which we have provided for them. Their food was cheap, their clothes inexpensive, we have been enriched by the fruits of their labour; we have brought up our sons and our daughters and lived, many of us, in the enjoyment of luxuries . . . At our bidding they have undergone fatigue and labour; at our command they have perilled themselves on the ocean and hundreds and thousands have perished in the deep. And, in return for all these sacrifices, what do their children of the present generation demand of us?

The Government would not swallow Esten's far-reaching plan, but in 1839 the first general grant for education of white and black was made, and from then on, apart from a short period between 1860 and 1866, Government has continued to help education. In recent years more money has been spent on education than on any other government activity.

New Schools

In 1853 a new school was opened which was meant to carry out part of Bishop Berkeley's plan. The man behind it was the Rev

William C. Dowding, and his idea was to build a non-segregated school which would offer education not only to Bermudians but also to people of the West Indies.

Dowding obtained help from a number of prominent British sponsors, including the Archbishop of Canterbury, and with funds in hand came to Bermuda, hired a building, and started the school, which he called St Paul's after Bishop Berkeley's proposed institution.

The school started with mainly black pupils, with some white as well, but it came under severe attack from a number of prominent white people. Dowding was forced to return to England to try and obtain more financial support, but in 1856 the school was closed down.

Devonshire College

Earlier in the century an attempt was made to open a superior school for white boys, and what could be saved of the old Bermuda Company school lands were placed under a body of trustees. The trustees managed to sell much of the land, and devoted the proceeds to building a school in Devonshire. This was the Devonshire College. It was opened in 1829 but after a few years it proved to be a failure. Some of the buildings still stand however and are now part of St Brendan's Hospital.

Later on it was decided to turn the money over to two bodies of trustees: Body No. 1 to run a school for white boys and Body No. 2 to run a school for black boys.

The school for white boys became Saltus Grammar School, which opened in 1887 in Pembroke Sunday School and two years later moved to its own premises.

The Body No. 2 scheme ran into opposition, for many black people argued that the Devonshire College money should be kept together for an integrated school.

The argument dragged on for many years, but before it was resolved the Berkeley Educational Society had been founded with the idea of opening an integrated school. The society was formed by black people, but soon after its beginning it was joined by several white people, including the Rector of Pembroke, the Rev Mark James.

After a long struggle the Berkeley Educational Society succeeded in opening the school at Samaritan's Hall, Hamilton on 1st September 1897, with Mr George A. DaCosta as the first headmaster and twenty-seven pupils, one of whom was white.

For many years interest derived from Devonshire College Body No. 2 money was used to provide secondary school scholarships, but in 1933 the capital was turned over to Berkeley for additions and alterations.

Increase in Educational Activity

The period just before the present century was a time when many schools were started, among them Sandys Grammar School, the Bermuda High School for Girls, Mount St Agnes, Whitney Institute and St George's Grammar School. The schools started as white schools, and were built through the efforts of interested groups. Whitney, for instance, was built by neighbourhood fund-raising efforts. The school was partly built when a hurricane destroyed much of the work. But two neighbours, Mr and Mrs Whitney, gave money to make up for the loss which had been sustained, and the school was completed.

At the same time the Government was taking an increasing interest in education. An act passed in 1879 provided for the continuation of a Board of Education and an Inspector of Schools, but also added local parish school boards.

In 1881 there were twenty-one schools under the control of the Board of Education, which were inspected by a man who left his mark on Bermuda education, Mr George Simpson. Mr Simpson

Warwick Academy

was a tyrant, and ruled schools with such a rod of iron that he even specified what pieces of poetry should be learned. He continued in his post well into the twentieth century.

During the 1920s, '30s and '40s the school system grew only gradually, one of the most noteworthy events being the setting up of grants for teachers to train abroad in 1931. In the late 1940s this began to produce considerable fruit, giving great impetus to the development of a black professional class. Many teachers went on to other jobs and professions, but their start was gained through the teacher training programme.

The other big advance came in 1949 when, after a long struggle, free primary education was introduced. Education was still compulsory however only from the age of seven to thirteen. It was only in the 1960s that the period was lengthened, at first from five to fifteen years, and then to the present five to sixteen years. By then most children were being educated for longer periods, anyway.

Despite the teacher training programme, men and women were constantly brought in from abroad to provide enough teachers. They came mainly from Britain and the West Indies.

Howard Academy

From the mid-1930s on the only two schools giving secondary education to black children were Berkeley Institute and newly-opened Sandys Secondary School, which was only kept going through considerable struggles. Then, in the 1940s, came the battle of Howard Academy. The Academy was started in the middle of the decade when Mr Edward Skinner, a former headmaster of Cavendish School, started tutoring youngsters in his home. It was quickly discovered that there was a heavy demand for secondary education for students who were unable to obtain places in Berkeley and Sandys.

Parents banded together to enlarge the school, giving their labour to build additional facilities. The Government was asked for help, but showed little willingness. Eventually an area of land at Prospect and a stone building was provided in 1953, and parents added a surplus wooden building obtained from the Royal Navy Dockyard.

In 1956 the decision to build the Technical Institute—designed to replace the Dockyard apprenticeship scheme and the first post-war school to be officially declared bi-racial—on the Howard site meant another move. Wooden buildings and a nearby site were provided, and once more parents turned to and erected a new school.

By this time Government had come to appreciate the intense longing in the island for secondary education, and, with the spark provided by Howard, St George's Secondary School was opened, to be followed by others. These new secondary schools were not expected to produce college-entrance graduates, but in fact many of them did so and continue to do so.

The arrival of other secondary schools however, meant the end of the Howard scheme. In 1965 the small government grant was withdrawn, and Howard closed its doors. But many of the pupils, particularly those educated under the dynamic Mr Edward DeJean, have played important roles in the community.

Recent Developments

During 1965 also government support for racially segregated schools was withdrawn, although by this time a number of former white schools had dropped the racial barriers anyway. No black schools had formal racial barriers.

At the same time the Government decided that Berkeley, Saltus and Warwick Academy were to take special responsibility for college-entrance training, while the remaining secondary schools were to concentrate on vocational training. Secondary school placement examinations were used by the schools as a guide to the pupils they accepted.

The year before, the Bermuda High School for Girls had decided to leave the government system and become a private school. In doing this they joined a number of small schools and Mount St Agnes, which had never received outright government money. The High School left the system because they did not believe in the idea of separating likely college-entrance children from other children.

Some years later, in 1970, Saltus also decided to become a private school after a lengthy battle over the question of the Saltus primary section being run directly by the government instead of the Saltus trustees.

The question had developed out of moves to promote more integration of school populations by amalgamating mainly white primary schools with mainly black ones. Saltus primary was to have amalgamated with Northlands, a primary school (an idea suggested by the Saltus Trustees), but the Government felt the new school should come directly under the Department of Education. The Saltus trustees disagreed, and finally took the entire school out of the system.

In 1967 a brand-new school in premises built for the purpose, Warwick Secondary, was opened, and during the late 1960s the Government also decided to set up a separate centre for students working for General Certificate of Education 'A' levels, and the Sixth Form Centre was born. It met first in Pembroke Sunday School, then moved to a new school building at Prospect.

The establishment of the Sixth Form Centre was followed by a decision to turn the Technical Institute into another post-secondary school, following the lead already given by the Bermuda Hotel and Catering College.

The Hotel College traced its origins back to the Domestic Science Centre which was started in 1936 to provide training in looking after the home and also in hotel and domestic service. In the post-war years these functions were split. Home training was worked into the curriculum of all the schools and the Hotel School was set up to train Bermudians in hotel work.

In the last few years hotel science courses have been developed in the secondary schools.

In 1972 the three post-secondary schools were joined together and re-named the Bermuda College, giving Bermuda the equivalent of an American junior college.

Although the name 'college' seemed a little grandiose at the time the Bermuda College has in fact played an increasingly important role in Bermuda. It has set high standards for its principal courses, but at the same time has organised evening courses designed for the direct needs of people trying to improve their knowledge and skills in the arts, business and trades.

Full college-level education came to Bermuda in a limited way through the University of Maryland, which started and still operates night classes at the U.S. Naval Air Station, and through Queen's University of Canada, which runs correspondence courses, and college-level courses in Bermuda. In 1981 three U.S. colleges were operating courses at the base.

From time to time there are revivals of the old schemes to try and open a school to attract American and other outside students, but all such schemes which have actually started have failed after a few years of operation. Bishop Berkeley's dream remains to be fulfilled.

Parallel with the other educational improvements in recent times has come the establishment of schools for children with special handicaps. The first of these was Friendship Vale school for the physically handicapped, and now several other schools for children with other handicaps have been started. The quiet creation of schools of this kind has been one of the most important developments in education in Bermuda, providing hope for many youngsters who in times past faced desperate struggles to obtain an education.

NOTE

Education as it was in eighteenth-century Bermuda is described by Nathaniel Tucker in part of his poem, 'The Bermudian':

> *Near yonder hill, above the stagnant pool,*
> *My stern preceptor taught his little school;*
> *Dextrous t' apply the scientifik rod,*
> *The little truants shudder'd at his nod;*
> *Whene'er he came, they all submissive bow'd,*
> *All scann'd their tasks, industriously loud,*
> *And, fearful to excite the master's rage,*
> *With trembling hands produc'd the blotted page.*

Another view of education a century later is given by Mrs Georgianna Walker in her private journal. She arrived in 1863, and shortly afterwards wrote: 'The first news I get of any unusual event, such as a wedding or a funeral, is from the children, who rush home in a great excitement, saying school has broken up and teacher has gone to the "Sight" '

CHAPTER 23

Arts and Crafts

The Bermuda people have only developed two forms of art; architecture and Gombey dancing. That there are only two is not surprising; what is surprising is that any developed at all, for Bermuda is not a large place, and throughout its history it has been swayed by influences reaching it from North America, Great Britain and the West Indies.

Some of the original architectural forms sprang from the West of England, but local conditions and local materials brought important modifications. The first stone building of all however, the State House, erected by Governor Nathaniel Butler, was designed according to a different tradition. The Governor's idea was to make the house in the Italian style, out of stone, and to make the walls thick, to keep out the heat, and, doubtless, to withstand hurricanes as well. He decided to have a flat Italian roof, and to make that out of stone, too.

As it was a public building he apparently felt that it should have some decoration, and today the restored State House once again has a decorative entrance, and a flat roof.

The stone idea was an excellent one. Bermuda stone was fairly easy to quarry and cut into good-sized building blocks, and after a time the dimensions became standard; twenty-four inches long by six, eight or twelve inches wide, depending on where the stone was to be used, whether for the foundations, first floor or second floor.

But the flat roof was a poor scheme. Heavy rains easily penetrated the porous stone even when it was washed with lime, and a steep roof was needed to throw off the water. Chimneys were an important part of the building, for fireplaces were needed for cooking and winter heating, and at first, following the English fashion, they were placed inside the building. But during the long summer cook-fires had to be kept going, and the heat was a trial. That was apparently the way the characteristic outside Bermuda chimney developed, with its broad base leaving room for the fireplace opening inside the house, and then curving upward on the wall of the building up above the roof.

In the largest houses wealthy Bermudians followed the Virginia fashion of having the kitchen in a separate building because of the heat and smell problem and because of the risk of fire. There is even a record of a man renting his kitchen to another house.

Inside the house the steep roof tempted architects to use low walls and part of the inside of the roof for the ceiling, and so the 'tray ceiling' developed, with the walls just high enough for doors.

During the slavery period builders had to consider accommodation for the slaves, and many old buildings contain semi-basements, sunk partly below ground-level. These could be used for storage or for housing slaves, while the family lived on the upper level, reached by a sweeping set of stairs. These traditionally flared at the bottom, and are known as 'welcoming arm' stairs. Slaves did not always live in the basement; sometimes they had separate cottages.

The old houses we know today were not always particularly planned. Sometimes a couple setting up housekeeping would start with enough rooms for themselves, then add on additional rooms as their families grew bigger.

Houses often had a number of outbuildings, including the characteristic buttery. This building was designed with a high roof reaching a point, and usually surmounted by a stone ball. The high roof would help to keep the building cool, and thus it would be more suitable for storing food.

A similar design was often used for outdoor earth toilets, known as privies.

Water was always a problem, and the idea of catching water on roofs and leading it into tanks must have come early. Probably Bermudians, like most Western people, rarely washed themselves in times past, so the tanks were probably small. Quite when the old-fashioned round-top tank came into use is not known, but it was probably after many of the houses were built, for many of the tanks are of a fair size.

Most of the old houses had small windows made with thick frames to ensure strength against hurricanes. Blinds at first were made of boards fastened together, for jalousie blinds apparently did not reach Bermuda from the West Indies until the nineteenth century. They soon became extremely popular, providing safety for the glass windows and ventilation at the same time. Summer verandahs shuttered with jalousie blinds were added to a number of houses, and still dot the countryside.

Cedar trees appear to have helped dictate the size of houses. The difficulty of finding tall enough trees to provide stout beams over sixteen feet helped to limit the width of houses.

During the eighteenth century Bermuda houses often developed graceful lines and proportions, but the nineteenth century saw builders falling under the influence of Victorian artistic ideas. In Britain and America it was a time when the development of factories for making a wide variety of objects began to help large numbers of people to obtain decorative material, which in turn led to many fresh architectural fancies. Some products of this age will withstand the test of time, but others are unattractive.

Until recent times most buildings in Bermuda were painted with lime wash. The lime, also used for mortar, was made in Bermuda by cooking limestone rock over a slow-burning fire.

Our own century to a certain extent has seen a return to the simpler artistic views of the eighteenth century. Since the Second World War some of the ideas of modern architects have been introduced, producing some highly attractive buildings well outside the architectural tradition of the island, but also producing others of little merit.

Gombeys

Gombeys date back to at least the mid-eighteenth century, as is shown by the banning of their festivities after the trouble of 1761, but by the time of Harriet Suzette Lloyd's visit just before the end of slavery they were once again an exciting part of the Bermuda scene.

According to Mrs Albert Jackson, a dancer herself, the Gombey dances are an amalgamation of many different influences, from Africa, Britain, the West Indies and the American Indians.

At one time the Gombeys danced with high head-dresses made in many forms—a Noah's Ark, a house, a boat, an aeroplane—but more recently the height has been gained by using peacock feathers.

Costumes are still as colourful as they were when Harriett Lloyd saw them, and nowadays are often decorated with large numbers of small mirrors. Although marching bands no longer accompany the Gombeys, the military drums remain.

Most Bermudians are still entranced by the Gombeys, and turn out in large crowds when the sound of the drum, whistle and pounding feet are heard.

Crafts

Although original ways of creating artistic forms were strictly limited in Bermuda, the island through its history produced many able craftsmen. Woodworkers had the good fortune of having cedar to work in, for the wood takes on a deep lustre when carefully smoothed and polished. Time slowly darkens the cedar, so that some of the oldest pieces are almost black.

Examples of Bermuda silver.

It is a brittle wood which makes it difficult to use for delicate table and chair legs, but even this difficulty is overcome in some cases. Other woods were brought to Bermuda and used, notably mahogany, but also pitch-pine, which takes on a mellow light-brown hue with age.

Bermuda also produced a number of able silversmiths, and today Bermuda silver is rare and valuable.

Was the Bermuda rig, and were Bermuda-designed ships a matter of an art or a craft? The question can be argued from either side. Certainly during the eighteenth century Bermuda vessels were noted for their speed which must have been the result of good designing; in those days this was done by a man with a knife who whittled a 'half-model' (the side of a ship from bow to stern stuck

Bermuda fitted dinghies carry on a long tradition
of boat-building on the island.

on a piece of wood). Some half-models have been preserved and can still be seen in museums.

The Bermuda rig still gets a workout on dinghy-racing days, when small, open boats, heavily overloaded with canvas and manned by a large crew, fight for special trophies. One man is the bailer and is constantly at work. If the wind drops the captain is permitted to reduce the number of his crew; naturally each man goes to the rear and dives off the stern, giving the dinghy a good hard push as he does so.

NOTE

Bermuda Boats   An English officer stationed in Bermuda in the last century was delighted with Bermuda sailboats, but their sailing qualities frightened some people. One day he offered to take an American ship captain from Ireland Island to Hamilton. 'It was blowing a fresh breeze, no more,' the officer wrote. 'Before the boat had got out of the camber [enclosed breakwater] a puff of wind caused it to lean over for a moment. Although the worthy skipper had just undergone the ordeal of a very rough passage from America, he almost lost his head with fright.

'He gave a positive shout of terror as he abandoned his seat on the hatchway. He was answered by a shout of laughter from two young fellow passengers of the army and marines. But Jonathan [a last-century English name for all Americans] recovered himself, and exclaimed: "I'm no coward, but I don't like to take risks." '

EPILOGUE

Bermuda Today and Tomorrow

We tend to think of history as something which happened long ago, but it is as much what happened in the last sixty seconds as what happened in the last 100 or 1,000 years . . . but there is a difference. Events which occurred 100 years ago can be seen as leading on to other events which make up the road a community has followed, but events in recent times cannot be seen in the same way. Although an election or another important event may be said at the time to be 'history-making' only the test of time will truly tell.

Therefore a person can only guess at the directions in which Bermuda has moved since the first edition of this book was written in 1972. This chapter discusses these apparent trends, and attempts to look at the future.

Economics

The tourist trade has maintained its importance since 1972, but the economy has been strongly boosted by the expansion of exempted companies (see page 182). These companies have put a premium on office and accounting skills for people in their own offices and for the local companies which support them—principally banks and legal firms. By 1981 the number of Bermudians going in for office work or improved training began to indicate to the Department of Immigration that the Government would have to allow employers to hire non-Bermudians for certain kinds of manual labour, for not enough Bermudians were willing to work in these ways.

The problem of bringing in people to carry out any kind of work is the small size of the island. Fear that Bermuda's population would outgrow the space available, so that the island was no longer a comfortable or pleasant place to live in, led the Government to press for family planning many years ago. Although families grew smaller, the process was a gradual one, and at the same time the growth of the economy led to many non-Bermudians being employed on the island so that the population continued to increase.

By 1981 family planning was working well. As there were fewer young people, school enrolment declined, and it seemed likely that more than one school would close down completely. A census listing all the inhabitants is taken every ten years, and in 1980 the population had reached 54,000, less than had been expected. In 1960 the population was 42,600 and in 1970 it was 52,330.

The Environment

The growing number of people and the amount of money available meant that Bermuda's building boom continued during the 1970s, a situation which caused deepening concern as more and more woodlands and fields became covered in houses. Many felt that unless the most careful measures were taken to guide development and defend open spaces, Bermuda would be an unattractive place in which to live, and also unattractive for tourists to visit.

The Bermuda National Trust, formed in 1970 as the successor to the Bermuda Historical Monuments Trust, undertook the challenge of presenting this point of view. Membership of the organisation went up from a few hundred to two thousand in eight years. This encouraged the Government to impose stricter planning laws, and there was greater recognition that Bermuda's remaining open space was very precious.

One peak in the National Trust's history was the publication in

1981 of *Bermuda's Delicate Balance*, a book which surveyed the island from many points of view and warned of the dangers Bermudians faced.

One chapter gave careful scrutiny to the tourist trade, because it was felt that if the numbers of tourists visiting Bermuda became too large the pressures of too many people would make life much more uncomfortable even if the number of residents remained the same. At the same time if the economy declined there would also be unhappiness as people were deprived of the new comforts to which they had become accustomed.

One of these comforts is the motor car. The rule that only one car can be licensed for each home, whether a house or an apartment, has recently led to young people just starting work deciding that they are no longer willing to live with their parents, but want an apartment of their own. This in turn has brought increased pressure for more buildings. Other pressure has come from persons brought in to help run and service exempted companies, so that housing confronts the Bermudian of the early 1980s as a serious problem, while the question of widening the roads, detracting from the countrified look of the island, is also important.

Sport and Culture

Bermuda's wealth has also affected two other areas of island life. For much of this century Bermuda yachtsmen have competed with foreign sailors both here and abroad, and Bermuda has sent contingents to the Olympics ever since the end of the Second World War, except for the Moscow Games which were boycotted by many western countries.

But in recent times more Bermudians have played for their country in international competitions in an increasing variety of sports, sometimes surprising far larger countries by their highly competitive play.

Although sport appeals to many more Bermudians than cultural activities such as exhibitions of paintings, serious plays and concerts of classical music, nevertheless interest has grown in these areas as well. The most notable achievement is the Bermuda Festival. With Mr John Ellison as its first chairman, the Festival quickly grew into an established part of the winter season and has encouraged a number of youngsters to try for a career in the performing arts, always a difficult and uncertain undertaking. In other fields more people are struggling to succeed with the camera or the artist's brush.

Religion

Religious activities have also grown, and one or two new Christian sects have appeared. In addition a small but strong congregation of Muslims has become well established, and a number of young people have been attracted by the Rastafarian sect which was founded in Jamaica and worships the late Emperor Haile Selassie (Ras Tafari).

The Family

During this past decade many Bermuda families, in common with families in most parts of the western world, appeared to be losing their unity. There were an increasing number of divorces, rising from 2.5 divorces per thousand marriages in 1970 to 5.5 per thousand in 1980. Children attempted to leave home earlier to live in their own lodgings and make their own life. The sense of neighbourhood unity appeared to lessen in many parts of the island, and fewer old people lived out their lives in their own homes or the homes of their children.

It is impossible to give all the reasons for this loss of unity. Increasing wealth almost certainly played a part; the requirement of a separate household for car ownership was another, and perhaps the individualism fostered by a successful capitalist economy played a part as well. Some people feel that many Bermudians became more selfish, wanting to have more things in their homes, and were less concerned about the troubles of their relations or their friends. There was less of the old sense of sharing good fortune—and bad.

The Future

By 1981 it seemed likely that Bermuda would be able to solve her population problem. A combination of fewer births and increasing care about immigration—allowing the employment of enough skilled persons to maintain Bermuda's economy and life-style and carefully controlling other immigration into the island—indicated that the increase in the island's population, which had gone up since the mid-1800s, was finally approaching a halt.

Racial harmony continued to improve, but the improvement seemed slower than the dramatic changes of the 1960s and early 1970s, and this led to a feeling that perhaps progress had not been made. Race continued to play an important role in the way that people thought about many subjects, and a conscious effort continued to be needed if Bermuda was to move toward a time when the colour of one's skin was unimportant.

A possible solution to the shortage of land lay in making new land on the reefs. But Bermuda would certainly face the danger of seriously damaging the fragile coral. Water which has too much sand drifting in it kills the delicate organisms which are the living part of the coral, a particular danger for Bermuda where, because the island is the most northerly place where coral grows in the Atlantic, coral growth is slow. The danger is well illustrated by Castle Harbour which is only just starting to recover from the dredging associated with the building of the airfield in 1941.

The cost of making land would be high. Expensive sea walls might minimise the danger to the coral. If the coral were destroyed the cost would be firstly a reduction in the number of fish and secondly the longer-term danger of the reef being eroded away.

A major problem for Bermudians remained the question of

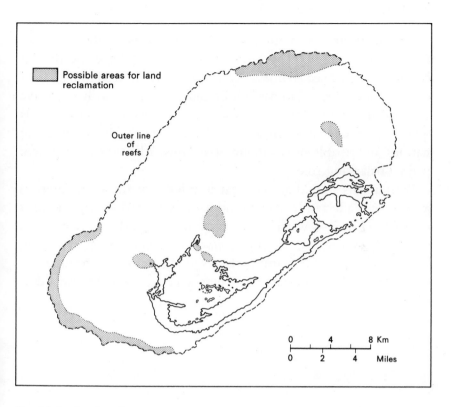

Possible land reclamation areas.

whether to obtain independence. The Bermuda people have always
been under the Union Jack, unlike many other British colonies,
and while the British Empire has only a little of its former glory,
it still gives a degree of safety for those who shelter under its wing.

Another important consideration for the many Bermudians who
travel to distant parts of the world is the security of knowing that
Britain maintains a vast network of consuls who help British subjects in trouble. For Bermuda foreign representation would be
expensive and could cover only a few cities. At present the Government's only overseas cost is maintaining Bermuda tourist offices in
a few major American and Canadian cities and in London.

Bermuda remains important in a strategic sense, although long-range aircraft capable of carrying heavy loads have meant that command of the sea is of less value in war than it used to be. However, while an American base on Bermuda has a primarily defensive role for the safety of the United States, a Russian base on Bermuda would be an offensive threat to the United States. These two great nations are capable of squabbling over this Atlantic speck; Britain plays a balancing role.

Bermudians should always bear in mind that this community is a small one, affected by events and nations around it. Our motto is *Quo Fata Ferunt*—'Where the fates lead us'—and this remains as true today as it was for the *Sea Venture's* crew and passengers when, by a stroke of good fortune, they sighted Bermuda through the ocean spray and set in train the events which led to the present day.

Bibliography

Books in Print

Ann B. Brown and Jean M. Outerbridge, *Bermuda Houses and Gardens*, Garden Club of Bermuda, 1979.

William M. Cox, *Bermuda Constitutional Documents*, published by the author, 1970.

Elizabeth W. Curtis, illustrated by Diana Amos, *Bermuda—A Floral Sampler*, published by the author, 1978.

Stuart J. Hayward, Vicki Holt Gomez, Wolfgang Sterrer, editors, *Bermuda's Delicate Balance*, Bermuda National Trust, 1981.

Bryden Bordley Hyde, *Bermuda's Antique Furniture and Silver*, Bermuda National Trust, 1971.

Sister Jean de Chantal Kennedy, *Biography of a Colonial Town*, Bermuda Bookstores, 1961.

Major General Sir J. H. Lefroy, *Memorials of the Bermudas,* Bermuda Historical Society and Bermuda National Trust, 1981 (in two volumes).

Frank E. Manning, *Black Clubs in Bermuda*, Cornell University Press, Ithaca and London, 1973.

Louis S. Mowbray, *A Guide to the Reef, Shore and Game Fish of Bermuda*, third edition, 1976.

Nellie E. Musson, *Mind the Onion Seed*, Mussons, Bermuda, 1979.

Cyril O. Packwood, *Chained on the Rock*, Eliseo Torres and Sons, New York, and Baxters Ltd, Bermuda, 1975.

Cyril O. Packwood, *Detour-Bermuda, Destination—U.S. House of Representatives*, Baxters Ltd, 1977.

Dr Kenneth E. Robinson, *Heritage*, Macmillan Education and Berkeley Educational Society, Bermuda, 1979.

James E. Smith, *Slavery in Bermuda*, Vantage Press, New York, Washington, Atlanta, Hollywood, 1976.

Captain John Smith, *The Generall Historie of Virginia, New England and the Summer Isles*, Johnson Publishing Co., North Carolina.

Lt Cdr Ian Stranack, R.N. (Retired), *The Andrew and the Onions*, Island Press, Bermuda.

Mrs Terry Tucker, *Bermuda's Story*, Bermuda Bookstores, 1959.

Mrs Elfrida L. Wardman (editor), *The Bermuda Jubilee Garden*, Garden Club of Bermuda, 1971.

William E. S. Zuill, *Bermuda Journey*, Bermuda Bookstores.

Books Out of Print

Nathaniel Lord Britton, *Flora of Bermuda*, Hafner Publishing Co., New York.

Bessie Gray, *A Bermuda Garden of Song*, Marshall Jones Co., Boston, 1927.

Dwight Franklin Henderson (editor), *The Private Journal of Georgiana Gholson Walker*, Confederate Publishing Co., Alabama, 1963.

Eva Hodgson, *Second-class Citizens, First-class Men*, Bermuda Union of Teachers.

Frank E. Manning, *Bermudian Politics in Transition*, Island Press Ltd, Bermuda, 1978.

Dr Kenneth E. Robinson, *The Berkeley Educational Society's Origin and Early History*, Berkeley Educational Society, 1962.

Mrs Terry Tucker, *Bermuda Today and Yesterday*, Robert Hale Ltd, London, Baxter's Ltd, Bermuda, 1979.

Dr Henry E. Wilkinson, History of Bermuda in four volumes, Oxford University Press: *Adventurers of Bermuda*, 1959 (revised edition). *Bermuda in the Old Empire*, 1950. *Bermuda from Sail to Steam* (two volumes), 1973.

Index

Index